"This book provides a framework ... spiritual interventions based on Is...... j........ dence (*Shar'iah*) with psychosocial therapeutic interventions. Covering both the theoretical and theological underpinning of religious coping from an Islāmic perspective, this text delivers an integrative approach which can be used in psychotherapy to ensure a more holistic process of healing and well-being. It outlines the positive and essential contributions that interventions rooted in Qur'ânic and *Sunnah* can make in terms of prevention, treatment, and recovery. Chapters focus on highlighting the importance of daily supplications and prayers, as well as other Prophetic remedies as part of a comprehensive, encompassing therapeutic plan for not only psychospiritual, but also physiological afflictions. This book is an accessible guide to using Islāmic spiritual interventions in therapeutic practice for mental health practitioners, trainees, and students of Islāmic psychology."

Bagus Riyono, *President of the International Association of Muslim Psychologists (IAMP)*

Integrating Spiritual Interventions in Islāmic Psychology

This book provides Islāmic psychology practitioners a framework on integrating evidence-based approaches of spiritual interventions based on Islāmic jurisprudence (*Shar'iah* with therapy).

Covering both the theoretical and theological underpinnings of religious coping from an Islāmic perspective while also serving as a practical guide, this text delivers an integrative approach which can be used in psychotherapy to ensure a more holistic process of healing and well-being. It outlines the positive and essential contributions that interventions rooted in Qur'ânic and *Sunnah* evidence can make in terms of prevention, treatment, and recovery, describing a wide variety of practices and beliefs. Chapters focus on highlighting the importance of daily supplications and prayers, as well as other Prophetic remedies as part of a comprehensive, encompassing therapeutic plan for not only psycho-spiritual, but also physiological afflictions.

This book provides all Muslim mental health practitioners, trainees, and students as well as healthcare workers in Muslim communities with an accessible guide to using Islāmic spiritual interventions in therapeutic practice.

Juraida Latif is a psychologist and has 13 years of lecturing experience. Juraida is the director of The South African Institute of Islamically Integrated Wellness. She is a trained and practicing Islāmic psychology practitioner, having completed courses in Turkey and the United Kingdom, and an Associate Fellow of the IAIP. Her focus is on Islāmic counselling incorporating ruqyah and *Sunnah*-based wellness techniques.

Shaakirah Dockrat-Boda is a psychologist and director of The South African Institute of Islamically Integrated Wellness. She has 16 years of consulting experience and is a trained and practicing Islāmic psychology practitioner, having completed courses in Turkey and the United Kingdom, and is an Associate Fellow of the IAIP. Her focus is on Islamically integrated coun-selling and therapeutic applications.

G. Hussein Rassool is a professor of Islāmic psy-chology at the Centre for Islāmic Studies and Civilisations, Charles Sturt University, Australia. He is the director of studies at the Department of Islamic Psychology, Psychotherapy and Counselling,

Al Balagh Academy and Chair of Al Balagh Institute of Islamic Psychology Research. Fellow of the International Association in Islamic Psychology and Fellow of the Royal Society of Public Health.

Focus Series on Islāmic Psychology

Series Editor: Professor Dr. G. Hussein Rassool, Professor of Islāmic Psychology

About the Series

In contemporary times, there is increasing focus on the need to adapt approaches of psychology, counselling psychology and psychotherapy to accommodate the integration of spirituality and psychology. With the increasing focus on the need to meet the wholistic needs of Muslims, there was a call to adapt approaches to the understanding of behaviour and experiences from an Islāmic epistemological and ontological worldview.

The aim of the Focus Series on Islāmic psychology and psychotherapy is to introduce a range of educational, clinical and research interventions relating to Islāmic psychology and psychotherapy that are authentic, practical, concise, and based on cutting-edge research. Each volume focuses on a particular aspect of Islāmic psychology and psychotherapy, its application with a specific client group, a particular methodology or approach, or a critical analysis of existing and emergent theoretical and historical ideas.

Each book in the Focus Series is written, in accessible language, with the assumption that the readers have no prior knowledge of Islāmic psychology and psychotherapy.

Integrating Acceptance and Commitment Therapy with Islamic Psychotherapy for Managing Chronic Pain (2024)
By Razia Bhatti-Ali

Integrating Spiritual Interventions in Islāmic Psychology: A Practical Guide (2024)
By Juraida Latif, Shaakirah Dockrat Boda, & G. Hussein Rassool

Integrating Spiritual Interventions in Islāmic Psychology
A Practical Guide

Juraida Latif,
Shaakirah Dockrat-Boda,
and G. Hussein Rassool

Routledge
Taylor & Francis Group

LONDON AND NEW YORK

First published 2024
by Routledge
4 Park Square, Milton Park, Abingdon, Oxon OX14 4RN

and by Routledge
605 Third Avenue, New York, NY 10158

Routledge is an imprint of the Taylor & Francis Group, an informa business

© 2024 Juraida Latif, Shaakirah Dockrat-Boda, and
G. Hussein Rassool

British Library Cataloguing-in-Publication Data
A catalogue record for this book is available from the British
Library

ISBN: 978-1-032-38393-4 (hbk)
ISBN: 978-1-032-38394-1 (pbk)
ISBN: 978-1-003-34482-7 (ebk)

DOI: 10.4324/9781003344827

Typeset in Times New Roman
by MPS Limited, Dehradun

Juraida Latif
Dedicated to the Muslim healthcare fraternity, every person struggling with psychological and spiritual affliction and the general Muslim population who will benefit from this book.

Shaakirah Dockra-Boda
Dedicated to every Muslim mental healthcare practitioner, educator, the broader Muslim community, and those who contend with spiritual and psychological affliction daily.

G. Hussein Rassool
Dedicated to Idrees Khattab ibn Adam Ibn Hussein Ibn Hassim Ibn Sahaduth Ibn Rosool Ibn Olee Al Mauritiusy, Isra Oya, Asiyah Maryam, Idrees Khattab, Adam Ali Hussein, Reshad Hassan, Yasmin Soraya, BeeBee Mariam, Bibi Safian and Hassim, Dr Najmul Hussein, and Mohammed Ali.

Abu Hurayrah reported the Prophet Muhammad (ﷺ) as saying: *If anyone pursues a path in search of knowledge, Alláh will thereby make easy for him a path to paradise; and he who is made slow by his actions will not be speeded by his genealogy* (Sunan Abu Dâwud).

Contents

Tables

Foreword

Islāmic psychology is an emerging discipline in psychological science that is currently becoming more popular around the world. Even though the ones who benefit most of the discipline of Islāmic psychology are Muslims, it can also apply to non-Muslims. The discipline itself is developing through an evidence-based scientific methodology as it integrates almost all schools of psychology in a dynamic and holistic manner.

One of the prominent figure in classical Islāmic psychology is Al-Ghazali. In his work that is titled "The Alchemy of Happiness," Al-Ghazali describes the dynamic of the self and warns us that we have to be cautious about the drives within ourselves that can be dominated by lust and aggression. However, Al-Ghazali also prescribes the self-discipline that can help us to control these drives which is through the knowledge of the self, the knowledge about Alláh, the understanding of the meaning of this world, and the understanding of the meaning of the hereafter. This prescription will make an individual experience happiness. As we are fully aware, the topic of happiness is one of the core discourse in positive psychology. Another important discourse in positive psychology is called flourishing. The meaning of flourishing in the discipline of positive psychology has similar meaning with *Tazkia* in the discourse of Islāmic psychology. *Tazkia* is very familiar to Muslim scholars, and usually the word *Tazkia* is related to the word *nafs*. *Nafs* has multidimensional meaning. It can mean the soul, the individual, and it also means human life and breath as the manifestation of life. If we look at the dictionary, the word that has similar meaning with the *nafs* is psyche. Based on the Merriam-Webster dictionary, psyche means the soul, the mind, and also the breath of human life. This fact shows that Islāmic psychology and the discipline of psychology are very closely related. Therefore, Islāmic psychology actually is not alien to the discipline of psychology since the beginning.

Considering the facts that are described above, the book "Integrating Spiritual Interventions in Islāmic Psychology: A Practical Guide" is very important that will leverage a theory of Islāmic psychology to the level of more practical that can benefit the Islāmic practitioners. The one divining contribution of Islāmic psychology to the modern discipline of psychology as the recognition of Alláh the Almighty in understanding the dynamics of human psyche and also the solution of any psychological problem. This is what spirituality means in Islāmic psychology.

I am very confident that this book will bring significant benefits not only for the Muslim *Ummah* but also for humanity as a whole. I wish that those who need to expand their perspective on psychology can learn from this book. May Alláh bless our effort to understand ourselves and our life deeper and more comprehensively. Ameen

Bagus Riyono
President of the International Association
of Muslim Psychologists (IAMP)

Preface

The primary goal of the Focus Series on Islāmic psychology and psychotherapy is to present authentic and research-based themes in the field. It aims to enhance understanding of the complexities associated with Islāmic psychology and make it more accessible to educators, clinical psychologists, psychotherapists, and counsellors. One specific book in the series, "Integrating Spiritual Interventions in Islāmic Psychology: A Practical Guide," explores spiritual interventions within the Islāmic paradigm. This book responds to the growing need to address the holistic needs of Muslims, offering evidence-based guidance on integrating spiritual interventions in Islāmic psychotherapy.

The interest in addressing mental health issues within various racial and religious communities, including Muslim societies, has been on the rise. These communities seek counselling and psychotherapy approaches that align with their religious beliefs. Muslim psychologists practicing within mainstream paradigms have noticed a shift towards incorporating faith and sacred practices into therapeutic interventions. Many Muslim clients, who hold strong religious beliefs, often turn to God for guidance and support when dealing with mental health issues. Islāmic psychologists understand that mental health problems are complex and can involve factors beyond psychological or physiological imbalances, including the spiritual dimension.

This book emphasises the need to extract profound psychological insights from religious traditions for the benefit of all. The authors argue that acts of remembrance and supplication, Prophetic medicine, and incantations are effective psycho-spiritual tools within Islāmic psychology. They aim to dispel misconceptions and highlight the versatility of these interventions. While the book addresses issues related to *jinn* possession, the evil eye, and black magic, it also covers other relevant topics in Islāmic psychology.

There is currently a lack of suitable handbooks covering the content proposed in this book. Existing literature on spiritual healing often targets the general public or focuses mainly on specific issues. This book aims to provide Islāmic psychologists and Muslim mental health practitioners with a theoretical foundation and practical guidance on integrating spiritual interventions into therapy, regardless of the underlying causes being spiritual, psychological, physiological, or a combination of all three. It fills a gap in the market for a practical guide and handbook addressing this specific theme.

The content promotes an integrative approach that can be applied within psychotherapeutic practice, ensuring a holistic approach to healing and well-being. It discusses the challenges faced by Muslims worldwide, including psycho-spiritual afflictions, religious coping from an Islāmic perspective, and the significance of supplications and Prophetic remedies as spiritual interventions. It concludes by discussing the role of Islāmic psychotherapists and mental healthcare practitioners in adopting a holistic approach. The book is written in a manner accessible to Muslim mental health practitioners, Islāmic psychologists, academics, and non-academics without assuming any prior knowledge in the field.

The book sets out the following objectives:

- To offer a comprehensive exploration of spiritual afflictions and the corresponding interventions.
- To maintain a global and multidisciplinary perspective on the subject.
- To cater to the specific needs of Muslim psychologists and practitioners.
- To raise awareness of this topic's relevance in the context of Islāmic psychotherapy and counselling.
- To demonstrate the connection between spiritual afflictions and their impact on mental health.
- To draw on authoritative sources, including Qur'ânic verses, authentic *Hadīth*, and guidance from respected scholars.

The book's significance lies in its appeal to a diverse audience interested in understanding spiritual afflictions and interventions within an Islāmic framework. It is particularly valuable for professionals in psychology, including clinical psychologists, practitioners of Islāmic psychology, healthcare workers in Muslim communities, counsellors, academics, and individuals dealing with spiritual afflictions. Moreover, it serves as a relevant resource for undergraduate students in health and social care sciences, especially those studying psychology and psychiatry, as well as the broader Muslim community.

While the book may also be of interest to Islāmic scholars and religious leaders, its primary purpose is to provide foundational knowledge rather than in-depth training for those actively practicing as spiritual healers. Instead, it aims to equip Muslim mental health practitioners and students with essential theoretical information rooted in Qur'ânic and *Sunnah* evidence, enabling them to identify potential concerns and recommend evidence-based approaches that empower clients in their mental health journey. The goal is to facilitate an understanding of spiritual interventions within the context of psychological therapy.

Acknowledgements

Juraida Latif
All praise and thanks be to Alláh, Lord and Sustainer of the heavens and earth, for favouring me with this opportunity and allowing me to fulfil this heartfelt dream, and may the peace and blessings of Alláh, shower upon our Prophet Muhammad (ﷺ), his family, and his companions. I ask Alláh Almighty to accept this from me and forgive me for any shortcomings. The Prophet (ﷺ) said, "He who does not thank the people, is not thankful to Alláh" (Abu Dawud).

I wish to extend my profound gratitude to my deeply respected mentor and co-author, Professor G. Hussein Rassool. His steadfast dedication to the field of Islámic psychology is truly commendable. I am eternally grateful for his patience, belief in me, and unwavering support throughout the journey of writing this book. May Alláh preserve him and allow him to reap the rewards of his efforts in both worlds.

I am forever indebted to my co-author and friend who is more of a sister, Shaakirah Dockrat-Boda. Without her, the dream of penning this book would have remained unrealised. Her tenacity and dedication throughout this journey will always be etched in my heart among our most treasured moments together. May Alláh accept this from us and grant her the reward for her pure intentions.

To the editorial team and publishers, I am truly grateful for their input and professional flair.

I would also like to extend my deepest thanks to the clients who so willingly gave their consent to share their story, as well as everyone who has shared their experiences regarding Islamically integrated therapies.

I would also like to specifically extend my deepest appreciation and affection to my father, husband, children, and the wider family circle for their unwavering patience and unparalleled support throughout this endeavour. To my friends, you know who you are, your constant encouragement and backing have not gone unnoticed or uncherished. I love you all for the pleasure of Alláh. I am deeply grateful to the scholars of *Aqeedah* and *Ruqyah-ash-Shar'iah* from whom I have gained invaluable knowledge, as well as the practitioners in Islāmic psychology who have illuminated our comprehension of the human soul through an Islāmic lens. Their invaluable insights have greatly enhanced my research and practice in this domain.

I beseech Alláh, The Most Exalted and Magnificent, to accept this work as a sincere effort done solely for Him, and to forgive any imperfections encountered during its compilation. Any errors within are from *shaytan* and me, and Alláh and His Messenger (ﷺ) are free from it. May Alláh allow this book to benefit all those who read it. May He bestow healing upon all those grappling with trials and tribulations in all its forms.

Shaakirah Dockrat-Boda

All praise belongs to Alláh, and may the peace and blessings of Alláh shower upon our Prophet Muhammad (ﷺ), his family, and his companions. I begin by expressing my deepest gratitude to Alláh, the Most Merciful and Most Compassionate, for His unwavering guidance and blessings throughout my journey in the field of Islāmic psychology. His wisdom has illuminated my path and allowed me to delve into the profound insights of the human psyche from an Islāmic perspective.

I would like to extend my heartfelt thanks to my esteemed mentor and co-author, Professor G. Hussein Rassool, whose profound knowledge, guidance, support, and encouragement have been instrumental in enriching my understanding of the subject matter and that of Islāmic psychology. Your wisdom and dedication to the field have been a constant source of inspiration. Your patience and trust demonstrated while co-authoring this book is a testament to the dedication to the shared vision of this book.

I would also like to extend my deepest gratitude to my co-author and dear friend Juraida Latif who brought a wealth of insight into this endeavour, enriching it with her unique perspective and contributions. Your tireless efforts and collaborative spirit were instrumental in shaping the content of this book. I am forever thankful to the Almighty for allowing us this opportunity to co-author this book together and to be a part of the realisation of your dream.

I am deeply appreciative to the editing team and publishers for their valuable input and professional expertise.

Beyond the professional collaborations, I am truly indebted to my husband for his endless patience, understanding, and unconditional support during the challenging phases of this research which have been integral to its success, and to my family and friends for their moral support and encouragement. Their faith in my pursuits has been a driving force behind my commitment to this field.

I would also like to express my profound gratitude to the clients who generously granted permission to share their stories and to all those who have shared their insights on their journey with spiritual affliction and Islamically integrated therapies.

I am deeply grateful to the scholars and practitioners in the field of Islāmic psychology who have paved the way for our understanding of the human soul from an Islāmic perspective. Their contributions have enriched my research and practice in this area.

I attribute any merit and correctness within this book entirely to the grace of Allāh, while I take sole responsibility for any errors. I humbly implore Allāh's forgiveness for any unintended deficiencies in the content of this book and pray that this endeavour proves beneficial to all its readers and those interested in the content of this book. May Allāh provide relief and healing to all those facing difficulties and challenges with psychological, physical, and spiritual affliction.

G. Hussein Rassool
All praise is due to Allāh and may the peace and blessings of Allāh be upon our Prophet Muhammad (ﷺ), his family, and his companions.

I would like to thank Grace McDonnell Publisher at Routledge, for her valuable and constructive suggestions during the development of the proposal, and during the process of writing. To Sara Hafeez, Editorial Assistant at Routledge for her constant support in this endeavour.

I am thankful to my beloved parents who taught me the value of education. I owe my gratitude to Mariam, Idrees Khattab, Ibn Adam Ali Hussein, Ibn Hussein Ibn Hassim, Ibn Sahaduth Ibn Rosool Al Mauritiusy, Adam Ali Hussein, Reshad Hasan, Yasmin Soraya, Isra Oya, Asiyah Maryam, Nabila Akhrif, Nusaybah Burke, Musa Burke, Dr Najmul Hussein, and Mohammed Ali for their unconditional love and who provided unending inspiration.

I would like to acknowledge the contributions of my teachers who enabled me, through my own reflective practices, to understand authentic Islām, and from their guidance to follow the right path of the Creed of *Ahlus-Sunnah wa'l-Jama'ah*. Finally, whatever benefits and correctness you find within this book are out of the Grace of Allāh, Alone, and whatever mistakes you find are mine alone. I pray to Alláh to forgive me for any unintentional short-comings regarding the contents of this book and to make this humble effort helpful and fruitful to any interested parties.

Whatever of good befalls you, it is from Alláh; and whatever of ill befalls you, it is from yourself. [An-Nisā' (The Women) 4:79]

بِسْمِ اللهِ الرَّحْمَنِ الرَّحِيمِ

Praise be to Alláh, we seek His help and His forgiveness. We seek refuge with Alláh from the evil of our own souls and from our bad deeds. Whomsoever Alláh guides will never be led astray, and whomsoever Alláh leaves astray, no one can guide. I bear witness that there is no god but Alláh, and I bear witness that Muhammad is His slave and Messenger. (*Sunan al-Nasa'i: Kitaab al-Jumu'ah, Baab kayfiyyah al-khutbah*)

- *Fear Alláh as He should be feared and die not except in a state of Islām (as Muslims) with complete submission to Alláh.* (Ali-'Imran 3:102)[1]
- *mankind! Be dutiful to your Lord, Who created you from a single person, and from him He created his wife, and from them both He created many men and women, and fear Alláh through Whom you demand your mutual (rights), and (do not cut the relations of) the wombs (kinship) Surely, Alláh is Ever an All-Watcher over you).* (Al-Nisā' 4:1)
- *you who believe! Keep your duty to Alláh and fear Him and speak (always) the truth).* (Al-Aĥzāb 33:70)
- *What comes to you of good is from Alláh, but what comes to you of evil, [O man], is from yourself.* (An-Nisā 4:79)

The essence of this book is based on the following notions:

- The fundamental of as a religion is based on the Oneness of God.
- The source of knowledge is based on the Qur'ān and *Hadīth*. (*Ahl as-Sunnah wa'l-Jamā'ah*)
- Empirical knowledge from sense perception is also a source of knowledge through the work of classical and contemporary Islāmic scholars and research.
- Islām takes a holistic approach to health: physical, psychological, social, emotional, and spiritual health cannot be separated.
- Muslims have an Islāmic or Qur'ânic worldview different from the Western' oriented worldview.
- It is a sign of respect that Muslims would utter or repeat the words 'Peace and Blessing Be Upon Him' after hearing (or writing) the name of Prophet Muhammad (ﷺ).

Note

1 The translations of the meanings of the verses of the Qur'ān in this book have been taken, with some changes, from Saheeh International, The Qur'ān: Arabic Text with corresponding English meanings.

1 Trials and tribulations of Muslims

Introduction

Islām is a religion with a monotheistic belief system, based on the teachings revealed to Prophet Muhammad (ﷺ) 1400 years ago and recorded in the Qur'ân. Muslims account for approximately 23% of the world's population, with the majority living in Asian-Pacific countries (Cifti et al., 2013). The global Muslim population is estimated to be around 1.6 billion people, and this number is projected to increase by about 35% to reach 2.2 billion by 2030, according to Pew Research Center's Forum on Religion and Public Life (2011). The Muslim population is both significant in number and geographically diverse. Muslims are not a homogeneous group, as they consist of indigenous and migrant populations in North America, Western and Northern Europe, and Australasia. This diversity challenges the perception of Muslims as a homogeneous group, as is often the case with Western orientalists (Rassool, 2019). "A number of socio-political occurrences both inside countries with large

DOI: 10.4324/9781003344827-1

Muslim majorities and externally have generated a multiplicity of political, social, economic and psychological problems" (Rassool, 2019, p. 12). There are various psycho-social challenges and spiritual diseases faced by indigenous and migrant Muslims living in the Western societies. The impact of September 11th and the associated discrimination, microaggression, Islāmophobia, harassment, hate crimes, violence, and anti-Muslim sentiment has increased the risk of psychological distress, including post-traumatic stress disorder (PTSD), anxiety, and depression.

In addition, many Muslim-majority countries affected by significant political, social, economic, and security challenges result in various forms of human suffering and devastation. Furthermore, the additional secondary psychological difficulties such as grief separation, acculturation, language barriers, lack of family support, and change in family dynamics all contribute to the dire and desperate mental health conditions in this environment. In addition to the many psycho-social challenges faced by Muslims globally, Muslims are facing further challenges as most Western scholarship and media have portrayed Islām and Muslims in terms of global terrorism, fundamentalism, fascism, and Islāmic authoritarianism leading to social exclusion, hate rhetoric, microaggression, and violence (Esposito & Ibrahim, 2011). To make matters worse, psychological problems are often stigmatised in Muslim communities, and individuals often suffer in unbearable silence.

The aims of this chapter are to highlight the trials, tribulations, and psycho-social, spiritual, and mental health challenges of Muslim communities on a global level. It will underscore research-based examples of challenges faced by Muslims from a biopsychosocial and spiritual lens. It briefly addresses the three categories of spiritual affliction and ends with a summary of the three types of hearts as well as their related treatment.

Trials and tribulations

Muslims, generally, will withstand many trials and tribulations throughout their lives. Alláh tests us with hardship and also prosperity in order to validate the sincerity of our faith. This is reflected in the following verse of the Qur'ân. Alláh says:

ٱلَّذِى خَلَقَ ٱلْمَوْتَ وَٱلْحَيَوٰةَ لِيَبْلُوَكُمْ أَيُّكُمْ أَحْسَنُ عَمَلًا ۚ وَهُوَ ٱلْعَزِيزُ ٱلْغَفُورُ

- *It is He who created death and life to test which of you are best in deed, for he is the Almighty, the Forgiving.* (Al-Mulk 67:2, interpretation of the meaning)

In addition, Alláh says in the Qur'ân:

وَلَنَبْلُوَنَّكُم بِشَىْءٍ مِّنَ ٱلْخَوْفِ وَٱلْجُوعِ وَنَقْصٍ مِّنَ ٱلْأَمْوَٰلِ وَٱلْأَنفُسِ وَٱلثَّمَرَٰتِ ۗ وَبَشِّرِ ٱلصَّٰبِرِينَ

- *And We will surely test you with something of fear and hunger and a loss of wealth and lives and fruits but give good tidings to the patient.* (Al-Baqarah 2:155, interpretation of the meaning)

According to the exegesis of Ibn Kathir, Alláh informs us that He tests and tries His servants; hence, He sometimes tests them with bounty and sometimes with the afflictions of fear and hunger (Ibn Kathir, 2003). This means that Muslims will endure many trials throughout life, such as being afflicted by disease, calamity, suffering oppression, injustice, and other trials and tribulations. Mus'ab bin Sa'd narrated from his father that a man said: "O Messenger of Alláh (ﷺ)!Which of the people is tried most severely?" He said: "The Prophets, then those nearest to them, then those nearest to them. A man is tried according to his religion; if he is firm in his religion, then his trials are more severe, and if he is frail in his religion, then he is tried according to the strength of his religion. The servant shall continue to be tried until he is left walking upon the earth without any sins." Trials and tribulations also have a purpose for Muslims as these could be a signpost that Alláh intends good for us. This is reinforced in the following *Hadīth*. It is narrated by Abu Hurayrah that Alláh 's Messenger (ﷺ) said, "If Alláh wants to do good to somebody, He afflicts him with trials" (Bukhari (a)). In addition, it is through trials and tribulations that our sins are expiated and we have the opportunity to perform good deeds. A'isha (may Alláh be pleased with her) reported: I heard Alláh 's Messenger (ﷺ) as saying: There is nothing (in the form of trouble) that comes to a believer even if it is the pricking of a thorn that there is decreed for him by Alláh good or his sins are obliterated" (Muslim (a)).

Psychosocial issues

Psychosocial characteristics or challenges, as defined by Vizotto et al. (2013), refer to the impact of social factors on an individual's mental health and behaviour, as well as the relationship between social and behavioural factors. Social factors, including peer pressure, parental support, cultural and religious background, socioeconomic status, and interpersonal relationships, play a significant role in shaping an individual's personality and influencing their psychological makeup. Individuals with psychosocial disorders may have difficulty functioning in social situations and struggle to effectively communicate with others. The symptoms of psychosocial disorders vary depending on the specific diagnosis. Besides disorder-specific symptoms, individuals with psychosocial dysfunction often struggle to establish and maintain close interpersonal relationships (Epperly & Moore, 2000).

Indigenous and migrant Muslims residing in Western societies encounter a range of psycho-social difficulties. Following the events of September 11th, anti-Muslim sentiment has increased, elevating the risk of psychological distress. Padela and Heisler (2010) suggested that this type of discrimination can also negatively impact an individual's level of happiness and overall health status. Furthermore, numerous Muslim-majority countries are experiencing significant political, social, economic, and security challenges, which result in various forms of human suffering and devastation. Among these challenges are the unprecedented displacement of individuals which is of particular significance. Due to war, conflict, persecution, torture, and ethnic cleansing within their homelands, refugees amount to 25 million worldwide, with the majority originating from Muslim-majority countries (Al Nuami & Qoronfleh, 2020). The authors further mention that the distress and trauma experienced, coupled with immigration and resettlement processes, increases the risk of refugees developing psychological problems such as adjustment disorder, somatisation, panic attacks, generalised anxiety, depression, and PTSD.

Acculturation, grief separation, language barriers, lack of family support, changes in family dynamics, industrialisation, the rise of divorce, and Islāmophobia are among the many psycho-social challenges faced by Muslims globally that contribute to poor mental health outcomes. These challenges can lead to feelings of isolation, depression, anxiety, and other mental health issues. The stigma surrounding mental illness in many Muslim communities also often prevents individuals from seeking help, further exacerbating the problem (Al Nuami & Qoronfleh, 2020). It is important to understand the interconnected contexts of racialisation, Islāmophobia, and discrimination in order to comprehend the realities of Muslims residing in Western nations. Racial groups are formed through the process of racialisation (Garner & Selod, 2015). The social construction of race is embedded in a power structure and is sometimes used to discount particular social groupings. Stereotypes, prejudice, and discrimination are all forms of racism that might occur overtly, covertly, purposefully, inadvertently, or even institutionally (Fish & Syed, 2020). It has been suggested that racial distinctions appear to be the result of the majority oppressing the minority (Kathawalla & Syed, 2021).

The common rhetoric is that the Muslim faith results in people being less committed to mainstream value systems in the United States and Europe, and from the backdrop of being a "phobia," Islāmophobia involves a sense of "justified fear" that allows discriminatory or racist tendencies towards Muslims for personal protection or survival of majority groups (Hervik, 2019). Fear of Muslims and Islām has been connected to anti-terror initiatives, such as the anti-Muslim laws in Europe and in the United States (Kathawalla & Syed, 2021). In the context of Islāmophobia, there has certainly been an increase in anti-Islāmic or Muslim hate-related incidents in the United States over the past 20 years. Studies including Muslims in the United States, Canada, and different parts of Europe have consistently found high rates of perceived discrimination directed to oneself or towards people they know (Ashraf & Nassar, 2018; Wilkins-Laflamme, 2018). Qualitative studies have also shown that Muslims report unique experiences of discrimination compared to other minority groups in the United States (Nadal et al., 2012; Sirin & Fine, 2007 as cited in Kathawalla & Syed, 2021) and Europe (Moffitt et al., 2018). Wilkins-Laflamme (2018) reports in a study among Canadians that non-Muslims reported the lowest rating towards Muslims living in Canada compared to other minority groups. These occurrences have facilitated the gross misrepresentation of Islām in the hearts and minds of many people and the global representation of Islām in the contemporary world.

Mental health problems

There are several mental health problems faced by indigenous and migrant Muslims living in Western-oriented societies. The post-9/11 climate globally, especially in countries in the Northern Hemispheres, has not only made many Muslims highly concerned with issues including discrimination, prejudice, threats, hate messages or harassment, microaggressions, violence, and Islāmophobia (Rassool 2019). There is evidence to suggest that the level of discrimination experienced (in all types) was associated with psychological distress (Moradi & Hassan, 2004), depression (Hassouneh & Kulwicki, 2007), PTSD (Abu-Ras & Abu-Bader, 2009), subclinical paranoia (Rippy & Newman, 2006), anxiety, and depression (Amer & Hovey, 2011). The findings from the study by Padela and Heisler (2010) showed that perceived abuse and discrimination after September 11 were associated with psychological distress, level of happiness, and health status.

In a research study by Hassan et al. (2016), it was found that there has been an increase in the number of Syrians experiencing psychotic symptoms due to various risk factors such as traumatic events, forced migration, and lack of social support. The largest psychiatric hospital in Lebanon has seen a rise in the number of Syrian patients over the years, with more severe psychopathology and suicidal tendencies. The International Medical Corps has treated over 6,000 people in the region, and around 700 of them have been diagnosed with psychotic disorders and the current living conditions have a significant impact on mental health (Hijazi & Weissbecker, 2015). In addition, the findings of a study by Mohammed and Abou-Saleh (2015) suggest that women dealing with loss are also prone to substance misuse and the misuse of prescription medications, leading to addiction.

Similarly, a Malaysian research study revealed that 26.6% of Muslim undergraduate students had depression symptoms, while 28.2% showed anxiety symptoms (Musa et al., 2015). A study in Pakistan demonstrated that doctors in emergency departments had higher levels of depression, anxiety, and stress, which were associated with job stress and burnout (Shah et al., 2018). Also, a study in the United States found that Muslim students experienced more stress, anxiety, and depression than non-Muslim students (Khalifa et al., 2017). The findings of a study by Rassool et al. (2023) to determine the frequency of depression, anxiety, and stress during COVID-19 among frontline healthcare workers (doctors vs. rescuers) in Pakistan showed that the majority of doctors reported a moderate level of depression (41%), extremely severe anxiety (30%), and a moderate level of stress (22%), while the majority of rescue workers reported a moderate level of depression (21%), moderate anxiety (14%), and extremely severe stress (10%). The authors concluded that the frequency of depression, anxiety, and stress is higher among doctors as compared to rescuers.

Research studies have also shown that Muslims globally are at risk of developing schizophrenia, PTSD, and suicidal tendencies. For instance, a study conducted in Malaysia found that 11.6% of Muslim university students had suicidal ideation (Musa et al., 2015). Another study conducted in Pakistan found that Afghan refugees who experienced war trauma had high rates of PTSD (Sajjad et al., 2019). Furthermore, a study conducted in Iraq found that individuals who had experienced war-related traumas had a higher prevalence of schizophrenia (Abbas et al., 2014). In many Muslim communities, there can sometimes be a cultural stigma surrounding mental illness due to misunderstanding or misinformation (Mirza & Rahman, 2015). Mental health issues are sometimes misconstrued as a sign of weakness or personal failing, which can make it difficult to seek help. This can further lead to untreated mental health issues and a greater risk of suicide (Khalifa et al., 2017; Karim et al., 2016). Muslims are also at a higher risk for experiencing trauma, particularly those who live in regions affected by war, conflict, or terrorism. This can lead to a range of mental health issues, including PTSD, depression, and anxiety (Shah et al., 2018; Sajjad et al., 2019). Many Muslim-majority countries have limited mental health resources and services, which can make it difficult for Muslims to access care. In addition, there may be a lack of culturally appropriate mental health services available to Muslim communities in Western countries

(Islam, 2018). These studies collectively suggest that Muslims globally are at risk of developing serious mental health issues and highlight the need for culturally sensitive mental health interventions.

Psycho-spiritual affliction

In Islām, there is an interconnectedness between the body, mind, and soul. Muslim professionals, particularly in psychological and medical practice, cannot deny the importance of the role of the soul (Abdussalam Bali, 2004). The spiritual afflictions affecting Muslims include the diseases of the heart, the evil eye, *jinn* possession, possession syndrome, religious scrupulosity (a form of obsessive-compulsive disorder), and black magic/ witchcraft (*sihr*).

Psycho-spiritual affliction and its impact on mental health and well-being in Muslim communities is a complex and nuanced one that requires careful consideration and exploration. While traditional psychological methods and approaches can certainly be helpful in addressing many mental health issues, it is important to recognise that some of these problems may have a spiritual dimension that requires an alternate kind of intervention (Shaikh et al., 2019; Nadeer, 2021). The psycho-spiritual paradigm recognises that certain spiritual afflictions, such as the evil eye, envy, *jinn* possession, and black magic, can have a negative impact on an individual's mental health and well-being. These afflictions are often overlooked or dismissed by Western approaches to mental health, but they are an important aspect from the lens of Muslim clients. Muslim psychologists and mental health practitioners should acknowledge the essential and necessary contribution that spiritual interventions based on Islāmic jurisprudence (*Shar'iah*) can make in terms of prevention, treatment, and recovery. The Islāmic spiritual tradition offers a wealth of practices and beliefs that can be analysed for therapeutic benefit. For example, the concept of submission to God (*tawakkul*) can be a powerful tool for coping with adversity and building resilience (A-Habeeb, 2013; Gadit, 2009; Shaikh et al., 2019). Evidently, the psycho-spiritual paradigm is an important aspect of the Muslim experience that requires careful consideration and exploration. By taking a holistic approach that considers both the psychological and spiritual dimensions of mental health, practitioners can help individuals achieve greater well-being and resilience.

References

Abbas, F. A., Al-Hashimi, A. H., & Al-Tai, A. R. (2014). Schizophrenia and war: A retrospective cohort study from Iraq. *International Journal of Mental Health Systems*, 8(1), 21.

Abu-Ras, W. M., & Suarez, Z. E. (2009). Muslim men and women's perception of discrimination, hate crimes, and PTSD symptoms post 9/11. *Traumatology*, 15(3), 48–63. 10.1177/1534765609342281

Abdussalam Bali, W. (2004). *Sword against black magic & evil magicians*. (C. Abdelghani, Trans.). London: Al-Firdous Ltd.

Al-Habeeb, A. A. (2013). Islāmic spiritual healing and psychotherapy. *Journal of Religion and Health*, 52(1), 1–17.

Al Nuami, S. K., & Qoronfleh, M. W. (2020). Mental health and psycho spiritual support for Muslim populations in emergency settings. *Journal of Muslim Mental Health*, 14(1). doi: 10.3998/jmmh.10381607. 0014.105

Amer, M. M., & Hovey, J. D. (2011). Anxiety and depression in a post-September 11 sample of Arabs in the USA. *Social Psychiatry and Psychiatric Epidemiology*. doi: 10.1007/s00127-011-0341-4

Ashraf, A., & Nassar, S. (2018). American Muslims and vicarious trauma: An explanatory concurrent mixed methods study. *American Journal of Orthopsychiatry*, 88(5), 516–528. 10.1037/ort0000354

Bukhari. *Sahih al-Bukhari* 5645. In-book reference: Book 75, Hadith 5. USC-MSA web (English) reference: Vol. 7, Book 70, Hadith 548.

Cifti, A., Jones, N., & Corrigan, P. W. (2013). Mental health stigma in the Muslim community. *Journal of Muslim Mental Health*, 7(1). 10.3998/jmmh.10381607. 0007.102

Epperly, T. D., & Moore, K. E. (2000). Health issues in men: Part II. Common psychosocial disorders. *American Family Physician*, 62, 117–124.

Espesito, J. L., & Ibrahim K. (2011). *Islamophobia: The challenge of pluralism in the 21st century*. New York: Oxford University Press.

Fish, J., & Syed, M. (2020). Racism, discrimination, and prejudice. In S. Hupp, & J. Jewll (Eds.), *Encyclopedia of child and adolescent development*. Wiley-Blackwell. 10.1002/9781119171492.wecad464.

Gadit, A. A. (2009). Role of faith healing in psycho-spiritual wellbeing of patients with psychiatric disorders. *Journal of Ayub Medical College Abbottabad*, 21(1), 78–81.

Garner, S., & Selod, S. (2015). The racialization of Muslims: Empirical studies of Islāmophobia. *Critical Sociology*, 41(1), 9–19.

Hassan, N. A., Mohamed, M. R., & Shah, S. A. (2015). Islāmic cognitive-behavioral therapy as a remedy for grief among bereaved Muslim clients in Malaysia. *Journal of Muslim Mental Health*, 9(1), 17–36.

Hassouneh, D. M., & Kulwicki, A. (2007). Mental health, discrimination, and trauma in Arab Muslim women living in the US: A pilot study. *Mental Health, Religion & Culture*, 10(3), 257–262. 10.1080/13694 670600630556

Hervik, P. (2019). Radicalization in the Nordic countries: An introduction. In P. Hervik (Ed.), *Racialization, racism, and anti-racism in the Nordic countries* (pp. 283–294). Cham: Palgrave Macmillan.

Hijazi, Z., & Weissbecker, I (2015). Syria crisis: Addressing regional mental health needs and gaps in the context of the Syria crisis. *International Medical Corps*: Washington.

Ibn Kathir, I. I. U. (2003). *Tafsir Ibn Kathir (abridged)*. Darussalam.

Islām, F. (2018). Islāmophobia and mental health: A systematic review. *Harvard Review of Psychiatry*, 26(5), 302–312.

Karim, A., Alam, M. T., Islām, M. A., & Habib, M. A. (2016). Prevalence and associated factors of depression among married Muslim women in a north-western district of Bangladesh. *Journal of Mental Health*, 25(5), 412–418.

Kathawalla, U.K., & Syed, M. (2021). Discrimination, life stress, and mental health among Muslims: A preregistered systematic review and meta-analysis. *Collabra: Psychology*, 7(1). 10.1525/collabra.28248

Khalifa, N., Hardie, T., & Latif, A. (2017). Exploring mental health and substance use amongst Muslim students in the United States. *Journal of Muslim Mental Health*, 11(1), 27–46.

Mirza, K., & Rahman, A. T. A. (2015). Exploring stigma and mental health help-seeking among Muslim immigrant women in Toronto. *Journal of Muslim Mental Health*, 9(1), 3–20.

Moffitt, U., Juang, L. P., & Syed, M. (2018). Being both German and Other: Narratives of contested national identity among white and Turkish German young adults. *British Journal of Social Psychology*, 57(4), 878–896. 10.1111/bjso.12268

Mohammed, T., & Abou-Saleh, P.H. (2015). Mental health of Syrian refugees: Looking backwards and forwards. *Lancet Psychiatry,* 2, 870–871.

Moradi, B., & Hassan, N. T. (2004). Arab American persons' reported experiences of discrimination and mental health: The mediating role of personal control. *Journal of Counseling Psychology*, 51, 418–428. doi:10.1037/0022-0167.51.4.418

Musa, R., Fadzil, M. A., Zain, Z., & Yusoff, M. S. B. (2015). Prevalence and factors associated with depression symptoms among undergraduate students in public universities in Malaysia. *Asia-Pacific Psychiatry*, 7(S1), 67–73.

Muslim. *Sahih Muslim* 2572g. In-book reference: Book 45, Hadith 65. USC-MSA web (English) reference: Book 32, Hadith 6241.

Nadal, K. L., Griffin, K. E., Hamit, S., Leon, J., Tobio, M., & Rivera, D. P. (2012). Subtle and overt forms of Islāmophobia: Microaggressions toward Muslim Americans. *Journal of Muslim Mental Health*, 6(2), 16–37. 10.3998/jmmh.10381607.0006.203

Nadeer, A. (2021). *The Ruqya handbook: A* practical guide to spiritual healing (1st ed.). Al Ruqya Healing. Independently published.

Padela, A.I., & Heisler, M. (2010). The association of perceived abuse and discrimination after September 11, 2001, with psychological distress, level of happiness and health status among Arab Americans. *American*

Journal of Public Health, 100(2), 284–291. 10.2105/ AJPH.2009.164954

Pew Research Center's Forum on Religion and Public Life. (2011). *The future of the global Muslim population.* Retrieved on 3 February 2022 from http://www. pewforum.org/The-Future-of-the-Global-Muslim-Population.aspx.

Rassool, G. Hussein. (2019). *Evil eye, jinn possession and mental health issues. An Islāmic perspective.* Oxford: Routledge.

Rassool, G. Hussein, Nawaz, K., Latif, S., & Mudassar, U. (2023). Depression, anxiety, and stress among frontline healthcare workers during COVID-19. *Journal of Islāmic International Medical College*, 18, 2.

Rippy, A. E., & Newman, E. (2006). Perceived religious discrimination and its relationship to anxiety and paranoia among Muslim Americans. *Journal of Muslim Mental Health*, 1(1), 5–20. 10.1080/15564 900600654351

Sajjad, S. J., Ali, S., & Yasin, A. (2019). Impact of war trauma on mental health of Afghan refugees living in Pakistan. *Journal of Ayub Medical College Abbottabad*, 31(2), 238–241.

Shaikh, S., Jones, N., & Farina, F. R. (2019). Islāmic spirituality: A foundation for well-being and resilience. *Journal of Spirituality in Mental Health*, 21(1), 1–20. 10.1080/19349637.2017.1416981

Shah, I., Zaidi, S. F., & Nadeem, M. (2018). The association of depression, anxiety and stress with job stress, burnout and life satisfaction among doctors in the emergency departments in South Punjab, Pakistan. *Pakistan Journal of Medical Sciences*, 34(5), 1205–1210.

Sirin, S. R., & Fine, M. (2007). Hyphenated selves: Muslim American youth negotiating identities on the fault lines of global conflict. *Applied Developmental Science*, 11(3), 151–163. 10.1080/10888690701454658

Vizzotto, A. D. B., de Oliveira, A. M., Elkis, H., Cordeiro, Q., & Buchain, P. C. (2013). Psychosocial characteristics. In M. D. Gellman & J. R. Turner (Eds.), *Encyclopedia of behavioral medicine* (pp. 1533–1534). Champs: Springer. 10.1007/978-1-4419-1005-9_918

Wilkins-Laflamme, S. (2018). Islāmophobia in Canada: Measuring the realities of negative attitudes toward Muslims and religious discrimination. *Canadian Review of Sociology/Revue Canadienne de Sociologie*, 55(1), 86–110. 10.1111/cars.12180

2 Psycho-spiritual afflictions

Introduction

In the realm of mental health and well-being, the intersection of psychological and spiritual aspects plays a significant role in shaping human experiences. Within this context, the concept of psycho-spiritual affliction emerges as a profound area that warrants exploration. Psycho-spiritual affliction refers to the intricate interplay between psychological distress and spiritual distress, wherein individuals experience challenges that encompass both domains simultaneously. It is essential for mental health professionals to have an understanding of religio-cultural differences, social customs, and values when working with Muslim individuals. They should recognise and respect the cultural and religious beliefs of their clients and tailor their interventions and treatments accordingly. This requires cultural competence and sensitivity, which can be achieved through training and education. Without such understanding and sensitivity, mental health interventions may prove ineffective and, in some cases, even harmful (Basit & Hamid, 2010).

DOI: 10.4324/9781003344827-2

Muslims may feel uncomfortable seeking psychological or psychiatric help to avoid conflicts with their understanding of religious requirements. The concept of psycho-spiritual affliction and its impact on mental health and well-being in Muslim communities is complex and nuanced, necessitating careful consideration and exploration. While traditional psychological methods and approaches can be beneficial in addressing many mental health issues, it is important to acknowledge that some problems may have a spiritual dimension that requires alternative interventions (Shaikh et al., 2019; Nadeer, 2021). By examining these multifaceted types of afflictions, we can gain a deeper understanding of the complexities individuals face when psychological and spiritual distress are intertwined. Furthermore, exploring the impact of psycho-spiritual affliction on mental health provides valuable insights into the potential pathways for intervention, healing, and holistic well-being. Through this exploration, we aim to shed light on the significance of recognising and addressing the psycho-spiritual aspects of affliction, ultimately fostering a more comprehensive approach to mental health and well-being. This chapter aims to delve into the nature and types of psycho-spiritual affliction and its effects on mental health and well-being.

Types of hearts

Al-Nu'man ibn Bashi reported that the Messenger of Alláh (ﷺ) said:

أَلَا وَإِنَّ فِي الْجَسَدِ مُضْغَةً إِذَا صَلَحَتْ صَلَحَ الْجَسَدُ كُلُّهُ وَإِذَا فَسَدَتْ فَسَدَ
الْجَسَدُ كُلُّهُ أَلَا وَهِيَ الْقَلْبُ

- *Verily, in the body is a piece of flesh which, if sound, the entire body is sound, and if corrupt, the entire body is corrupt. Truly, it is the heart.* (Bukhari, (a))

The heart is described as possessing life and death and is classified into three types according to Ibn al-Qayyim Al-Jawziyyah (Al Qahani, 2009; Rumaysa, 2003). The first type of heart is the correct heart also referred to as a sound and healthy heart and is one that is secure from all desires that oppose the command of Alláh and His prohibitions, and it is secure from all doubts that contradict what He informs. It does not worship anything other than Alláh. This is the only kind of heart that a person can present to Alláh on the Day of Judgement, and it will be the means of their salvation. This heart is also referred to as the truthful and sound (*salim*) heart (Al-Qahtani, 2009).

The second type of heart is referred to as the dead heart and lacks any signs of life. It fails to recognise its Creator and does not follow His commands nor engages in actions that please Him. Instead, it is consumed by its own worldly desires and pleasures, ignoring whether they are in line with the will of its Creator or not. This heart is enslaved by its carnal temptations and pleasures, oblivious to the fact that they may lead to the displeasure and wrath of Alláh. It is driven by its love for temporary things, and its desires have made it numb and indifferent to anything that contradicts falsehood (Rumaysa, 2003). The third type of heart is referred to as the diseased heart. It possesses life but is flawed in nature. It consists of two crucial elements, one leading it towards life and the other leading it towards death, and the heart follows whichever of the two is stronger. As a result, it either contains love, faith, sincerity, trust, and reliance on Alláh in matters that are vital to its survival. It also includes a love for worldly desires, prioritising them, and eagerly seeking them out. The heart is continuously being influenced by two voices: one calling it towards Alláh, His Messenger, and the afterlife, while the other calls it towards temporary, earthly matters. It responds to the voice that is closest and most influential at the time (Al-Qahani, 2009; Rumaysa, 2003).

In terms of trials and tribulations, and how the hearts manage this, Ibn al-Qayyim Al-Jawziyyah cited in Al-Qahtani (2009) mentions that anything that is directed to the person by shaytan, such as whisperings or suggesting to the heart any kind of suspicion and doubt, acts as a trial for the latter two types of hearts discussed above and serves to further strengthen the living, truthful, and sound heart. According to Al-Qahtani (2009), the heart can be treated by using the Noble Qur'ân. It serves as a remedy for doubt, disbelief, suspicion, and distress, while also serving as a guide for those who seek truth and mercy for believers through the benefits and rewards they receive.

Religious scrupulosity

Scholars and experts have shown interest in investigating the interaction between religiosity, guilt, and obsessive-compulsive disorder (OCD). A specific subset of OCD symptoms called religious OCD or scrupulosity is characterised by manifestations such as pathological doubt, religious themes, hyper-morality, excessive worry about sin, and engaging in overly religious behaviours, thoughts that centre around religious blasphemy, compulsive prayer, and engaging in cleaning or washing rituals (Yorulmaz et al., 2009; Himle et al., 2011). Moreover, there is evidence to suggest that the influence of religiosity on OCD-related cognitions may vary across different religions or even within different religious denominations, owing to different belief systems in religious doctrines and teachings (Rakesh et al., 2021). According to Rassool (2019), this psychological and behavioural disorder encompasses an excessive sense of guilt related to moral or religious concerns and accompanied by mental or behavioural compulsions, affecting individuals of different religious backgrounds. It is of utmost importance to note that the association between heightened religiosity, guilt, and specific obsessions and compulsions does not automatically imply that being highly religious leads to the development of certain OCD symptoms or an overall increase in OCD symptomatology. In fact, many individuals with OCD turn to religion as a response to alleviate their OCD symptoms (Rakesh et al., 2021).

Waswâs al-qahri is a commonly observed derivative of OCD in Muslim populations. Individuals who experience this type of affliction display extreme behaviours in their worship and daily activities, surpassing what is considered acceptable within the religion. For instance, Muslims with *waswâs al-qahri* may feel anxious or fearful that their ablution or prayer is somehow inadequate and must be repeated until they achieve their self-defined notion of perfection. The intensity of these intrusive thoughts, known as *waswâs,* can vary greatly and may appear very strong to those who are not familiar with the condition, giving the impression that the individual is engaging in these behaviours willingly (Rassool, 2019). From an Islāmic perspective, these unwanted thoughts are believed to be whispered into people's minds and hearts by the *jinn* (Rassool, 2019). Different types of *waswâs al-qahri* exist, including *waswâs al-qahri fee aqeedah*, which pertains to obsessions related to religious fundamental beliefs; *waswâs al-qahri fee taharah*, which involves obsessions related to purification; and *waswâs al-qahri fee kwaf min fuqdan al saytara,* which encompasses cognitive and affective experiences of losing control over one's life. Many Muslims who suffer from *waswâs al-qahri* are concerned about the implications of the disorder in terms of their accountability (Rassool, 2019).

According to the rulings of renowned Islāmic scholars (Rassool, 2019), there is a general consensus that individuals experiencing *waswâs al-qahri* will not be punished by Allāh. Imams or faith healers who possess religious knowledge from the

Qur'ân and *Sunnah* are required to be more attuned to differentiating between heightened religious practices and *waswâs al-qahri* in worship and pathological OCD. Further research is necessary within Muslim communities to gain a better understanding of this condition, as previous studies exploring the relationship between religiosity and OCD have predominantly focused on the Judeo-Christian tradition. This has implications for both clinical and spiritual intervention strategies (Rassool, 2019).

The evil eye *(ayn)*

The Almighty Alláh has created the human body and soul with different dispositions. As Muslims, particularly in psychological and medical practice, there is no denial of the importance of the role of the soul (Abdussalam Bali, 2004). There is a consensus among Muslim Sunni scholars that souls differ in terms of their natural disposition, inclination, and other aspects, and we should therefore strive towards purifying ourselves, particularly our souls (Abdussalam Bali, 2004). Regarding the soul, the Prophet (ﷺ) said, "The souls are like troops collected together, those that are familiar incline to each other, and those that are dissimilar are repelled" (Bukhari (b)). According to the scholar Badr ad-Deen al-'Ayni, this suggests that human beings are different based on their traits (*sifāt*), similar to an army that is made up of different divisions, battalions, and squads having their own distinguishing features (Al Ayni, 2001, as cited in Abdul-Rahman & Khan, 2020). Ibn al-Qayyim Al-Jawziyyah says that one of the benefits of this narration is that if an individual finds something in his heart against a good and righteous person, he should search for the cause of it, seeking to cease the ill-feeling (cited in Abdul-Rahman & Khan, 2020). Similarly, one can also harbour ill-feelings not due to any fault of the other person, but because of differences in our traits. Awareness of this could be very effective in an attempt to purify our hearts from ill feelings towards others.

In his book Fath al Bari, Ibn Hajar presents a range of perspectives within the Islāmic tradition concerning the concept of souls being attracted to one another. According to Imam al-Qurtubi, for example, souls possess distinct characteristics, and those with similar attributes naturally gravitate towards others in the same group. Abu Suleyman al-Khattabi suggests that this inclination might stem from souls having encountered each other before their earthly existence or from their shared qualities that forge a connection between them (Al-Asqalani, n.d). This information becomes important in terms of the understanding of the evil eye as it is something that is well known and there is no difference in opinion about its reality and effect (Nadeer, 2021). It is necessary to mention that jealousy in the general sense is not always a cause for the evil eye. It is also possible for a person to inflict themselves or those dear to them out of extreme admiration without seeking Allāh's blessing for it (possibly due to forgetfulness). This suggests that it is possible for the evil eye to result from a person who may be righteous and admires something even without having the desire to see that blessing removed from another person. The important component in preventing oneself from causing the evil eye is to seek blessing from Alláh with regards to the target of admiration (Nadeer, 2021; Abdussalam Bali, 2004). From the angle of the evil eye, we see that a soul that emanates jealousy can cause physical harm to the targeted person. It is therefore not surprising why Alláh in His infinite wisdom has revealed in the Qurân chapter 113 (Surah Falaq) that we seek refuge with Him from the evil of the jealous person (Abdussalam Bali, 2004).

Black magic/witchcraft (*sihr*)

The Arabic language is known for its depth and versatility, and it is not surprising that the word *sihr* has multiple meanings, both literally and technically. For the purpose of this chapter and in order to remain within the confines of our overarching theme, we will mention the definition by Ibn Al Qayyim Al-Jawziyyah who states that *sihr* consists of the effects of evil souls and the reaction of the resultant forces (Al-Jawziyyah, 1996). More simply, *sihr* is an agreement/contract set up between a magician and an evil *jinn* which obligates the magician to perform indecent acts of disbelief or polytheistic rituals in return for the assistance and obedience of the *jinn* in fulfilling the magician's request. Clearly, this suggests that the *jinn* will not assist the magician without receiving something in return (Abdussalam Bali, 2004). It is also evident from this explanation that there is a link between the involvement of *jinn* and the effects of *sihr*. It is beyond the scope of this book to go into the specifics of what these acts of disbelief entail, but the basic idea is that these acts constitute the worst forms of disbelief and disrespect to Alláh the Almighty. As Muslims, we cannot deny the existence of *jinn* or *sihr* because there is evidence for both in the Qur'ân and authentic *hadīth* in this regard. According to the scholars within the field of *ruqyah* (Islāmic treatment for spiritual affliction), magic can be cast for different purposes (Abdussalam Bali, 2004).

Jinn possession

According to Rassool (2019), the existence of *jinn* is established and affirmed in the Qurân. *Sunnah*, and the statements of the scholars. Muslims are required to firmly believe in the existence of *jinn*. Ameen (2005) argues that *jinn* are living beings with the ability to comprehend and are bound by commands and prohibitions. It is stated that "believers who affirm *tawheed* must acknowledge the existence of *jinn*" (pp. 41–42). Shaykh Al-Islām Ibn Taymiyyah asserts that the consensus of the Imams of Ahlul *Sunnah* wal Jam'ah, the larger body of Muslims adhering to the Prophetic traditions, confirms the fact that *jinn* can enter the body of a human (Rassool, 2019). Littlewood (2016) describes possession as the belief that an individual has been influenced or controlled to some degree by a non-human force, resulting in altered changes to their actions and identity.

There is also difference between magic and possession although both involve the *jinn*. However, mere possession without magic is the act of one or more *jinn* acting on their own accord. Magic on the other hand is a contract between the *jinn* and the magician which results in possession. Magic is stronger and more difficult to remove because the *jinn* are "forced" to remain within the person and are "tied" to the person through the contract. There is some evidence that enforcer *jinn* are sent to scare and intimidate them into remaining inside of the person (Muhammadtim.com).

Jinn possession can result due to different reasons. Among these reasons are the following, as presented in Table 2.1:

Table 2.1 Some reasons for *jinn* possession

Problems	Characteristics
Lust	Removing clothing without saying *Bismillah* or (seeking refuge in God), can attract lustful *jinn*. Engaging in impermissible material (like pornography) can increase vulnerability to *jinn* attacks.
Evil eye	*Jinn* can attack those already affected by the evil eye.
Revenge	Unintentionally harming *jinn* or their family (e.g., by throwing boiling water without Bismillah) can result in *jinn* seeking revenge.

(*Continued*)

Table 2.1 (Continued)

Problems	Characteristics
Mischief	Sometimes *jinn* may act maliciously without any reason.
Neglecting worship and heedlessness	Turning away from the remembrance of Alláh and being unmindful of protective morning and evening prayers can attract *jinn* interference
Attending un-Islāmic places and gatherings	Attending gatherings or places where pagan rituals or trances are performed can lead to *jinn* possession.
Black magic	Studying or practicing dark arts, visiting deviant healers, or playing with Ouija boards can make a person prone to *jinn* interference. People who are victims of black magic are also likely to have some type of possession.

Source: Adapted from: Nadeer (2021).

Types of possession

Possession exhibits diverse manifestations, characterised by distinct forms. Full possession denotes absolute control over an individual, resulting in impaired recollection of the events transpiring during this period. Partial possession, on the other hand, occurs when one or more *jinn* take up residence or traverse between specific areas of the victim's body. This phenomenon typically induces sensations of weightiness and pain and can lead to unexplained illnesses that elude medical

comprehension. Between states denotes an inter-
mediary state wherein the person remains conscious while coexisting with the presence of the
jinn. This experience may evoke confusion due to
the awareness of the *jinn's* presence and proximity
(Nadeer, 2021). Finally, transient possession tran-
spires fleetingly, confined to a particular time or
place before subsiding. It may arise during sleep or
in a semi-conscious state, characterised by sensations of chest pressure or heaviness akin to sleep
paralysis (Nadeer, 2021; Khalifa & Hardie, 2005;
Abdussalam Bali, 2004).

Spiritual afflictions in clinical practice

According to Al-Habeeb (2003), *jinn* possession can
present itself through a variety of strange behaviours
and unusual movements, which could be interpreted
as symptoms of various psychotic and non-psychotic
disorders. Rassool (2019) suggests that individuals
experiencing *jinn*-related possession "may exhibit
intense fear, psychological disorders, physical illness,
hallucinations, animosity between people, hysteria,
mania, property destruction, epilepsy, Tourette's
syndrome, schizophrenia, and even dissociative identity disorder" (p. 125). Additionally, true *jinn* possession may cause an individual to speak in different
languages or dialects that are incomprehensible
(Al-Ashqar, 2003).

   Begum (2016) points out that the distinction
between mental health issues and *jinn*-related problems can become blurred, particularly in cases
of psychosis, schizophrenia, and bipolar disorder.

This is because the symptoms of these mental health disorders may overlap with some of the characteristics of *jinn* possession, such as hearing voices, seeing things, paranoia, engaging in uncharacteristic behaviour, and experiencing irregular mood swings. This lack of clarity between *jinn* possession and mental health problems holds considerable importance in clinical settings, necessitating the awareness of mental health and Islāmic psychology practitioners regarding their patients' narratives. To enhance effective engagement with patients, Lim et al. (2015) suggested customising interviewing techniques to gather information about symptomatology, coping mechanisms, and the socio-cultural contexts related to patients' concerns. In cases where a dual diagnosis of *jinn* possession and mental health issues is identified, a collaborative approach involving multiple professionals is essential. This may entail consulting and seeking advice from local imams or faith leaders (Rassool, 2019). Below are examples of evidence-based case studies relating to *jinn* possession and mental health.

In a study conducted by Lim et al. (2018) in an outpatient setting, 118 patients were eligible for participation of which 41.5% were interviewed using a semi-structured questionnaire. Of the participants, 43% were positive that their psychiatric symptoms were caused by *jinn* affliction, whereas 27% thought not, and 31% were in doubt. No less than 87.2% had experienced some form of hallucinations during their lives. They also stated that among the proportion of eligible patients who chose not to participate (58.5%), many expressed a fear of stigmatisation or metaphysical repercussions if they spoke about the matter. The researchers concluded that the phenomenon of attributing mental health symptoms to *jinn* was much more common in Muslim patients than previously assumed. This emphasises the need for proper knowledge of Muslim explanatory models of disease.

In another study conducted by Abdul-Rahman and Khan (2020), the role of *jinn* possession in causing inter-psyche and intra-psyche conflicts was assessed using 34 symptoms of *jinn* possession derived from symptoms used by established *ruqyah* practitioners (practitioners who follow the Prophetic *sunnah* by reciting verses of Qur'ân and Prophetic duas in order to treat all kinds of ailments and diseases) globally. Out of the 1,088 participants, 530 were diagnosed as having *jinn* possession. The findings suggest that some mental disorders may also be cases of *jinn* possession or involvement. Abdul Rahman, Hussin, and Ridzwan (2021) conducted an exploratory study to investigate the possibility of *jinn* possession among patients who have been diagnosed with schizophrenia, bipolar disorder, and epilepsy using four case studies. All the patients had at least five significant symptoms of *jinn* possession and were on medication for their respective disorders. Thermal imaging of the patients was recorded using a thermal imaging camera to monitor temperature change before and after *ruqyah*, and the images were then compared. They found that parts of the body temperature for all four patients became hotter after *ruqyah*, suggesting that all of them have *jinn* affliction as this reaction to ruqyah is considered as a sign of *jinn* possession by experts in the field of *ruqyah*. This suggests that certain individuals who have been diagnosed with mental disorders may have an underlying problem with *jinn* possession or other spiritual inflictions. Incorporating *ruqyah* as a supplementary therapy for such individuals may result in improved therapeutic outcomes (Abdul Rahman, Hussin, & Ridzwan, 2021).

Effects of spiritual afflictions

There are many symptoms and effects that are caused by spiritual afflictions. As a general rule, if the cause of any ailment or distress is "idiopathic," i.e., has unknown medical causes, or if medical intervention shows little or no improvement, the likelihood of a spiritual affliction (one, two, or a combination of all three) should not be ruled out. Although there are multiple symptoms and effects of the evil eye, black magic, and *jinn* possession, for the purposes of this book, the focus will be limited to those related to psychological and neurological ill-health (Rassool, 2019). The symptoms and effects of the evil eye, black magic, and *jinn* possession are presented in Tables 2.2, 2.3, and 2.4.

Preventative and treatment approaches with regards to spiritual affliction will be covered under the chapters of fortification (*adkhaar*) and pre-scribed Islāmic incantation (*ruqyah-ash-Shar'iah*).

Table 2.2 Symptoms and effects of the evil eye

- Poor interpersonal relationships
- Hatred and anger towards family and relatives
- Inability to concentrate and confusion
- Nervousness, anxiety
- Depression
- Dissociative behaviour
- Homicidal impulses
- Suicidal impulses
- Feelings of futility
- Hallucinations and hysteria
- Feelings of shame
- Feelings of unworthiness
- Feelings of Inadequacy
- Obsessive-compulsive symptoms
- Hypochondria
- Delusion
- Withdrawal

Source: Adapted from Rassool, (2019).

Table 2.3 Symptoms and effects of black magic

- Sudden change in attitude from love to hate.
- Suspicion and exaggerating the causes.
- Distorted or poor perception of the person in dispute.
- Excessive love and passion.
- Massive changes in personality.
- Extreme desire and impatience to have sexual intercourse.
- A fixed object would appear to be mobile and vice versa.
- A small object would appear large and a large object would appear small.
- The false appearance of objects.
- Severe absentmindedness and forgetfulness.

(Continued)

Table 2.3 (Continued)

- Confused speech.
- Bulging eyes and deviation of sight.
- Restlessness and inability to do tasks.
- Disinterest in one's appearance.
- May have an epileptic fit or epilepsy.
- Love of seclusion.
- Absolute introversion.
- Constant silences.
- Antisocial.
- Frequent headaches.
- Quiet and constant lethargy.
- Nightmares.
- Auditory hallucinations.
- Whispering (*waswas*).
- Suspicious of friends and relatives.
- Paralysis of one part of the body or total paralysis.
- Extreme fear or anger.
- Extreme unawareness.
- Severe tightness in the chest especially between the mid-afternoon prayer and midnight.
- Anxiety during sleep.

Source: Adapted from Bali, (2004).

Table 2.4 Symptoms and effects of *jinn* possession

- Turning away from acts of worship and obedience to Allah.
- Erratic and irrational behaviour in words, actions, and movements.
- Becoming angry and weeping with no apparent cause.
- Idiopathic paralysis of a limb.
- Idiopathic seizures.
- Spending lengthy periods of time in the toilet and talking to oneself.

(*Continued*)

Table 2.4 (Continued)

- Idiopathic constant headaches which are not relieved by medication.
- Idiopathic sterility (and the psychological impact on both spouses).
- Depression.
- Suicidal ideation.
- Frightening nightmares.
- Talking loudly in one's sleep or moaning.
- Certain types of sleep paralysis, tightness in the chest, and panic attacks.

Source: Adapted from Ameen, (2005).

Conclusion

In conclusion, this chapter has provided an overview of the spiritual challenges faced by Muslims globally. It has also discussed how beliefs within the Islāmic faith affect the bio-psychosocial approach to managing psychological and psychiatric disorders. It further explained the overlap between the classification of symptoms and blurred boundaries between *jinn* possession and mental health. By examining spiritual affliction through an Islāmic lens, we gain insights into the spiritual dimension of human existence and the profound influence it can have on an individual's life and overall well-being.

References

Abdul-Rahman, Z., & Khan, N. (2020). Souls assorted: An Islāmic theory of spiritual personality. *Yaqeen Institute*.

Abdussalam Bali, W. (2004). *Sword against black magic & evil magicians*. (C. Abdelghani, Trans.). London: Al-Firdous Ltd.

Al-Ashqar, U. S. (2003). *The world of the jinn and the devils in the light of the Qur'an and Sunnah*. (Islāmic Creed Series, Volume3). Riyadh, Saudi Arabia: International Islāmic Publishing House.

Al-Asqalani, *Fath ul Bari. Al-Maktabah As-Salafiyya*. vol. 6, pp. 369–370. The subsequent statements by al-Qurtubi and al-Khattabi are cited by Ibn Hajar.

Al-Habeeb, T. A. (2003). A pilot study of faith healers's views on evil eye, Jinn possession, and magic in the Kingdom of Saudi Arabia. *Saudi Society of Community and Family Medicine Journal*, 10(3).

Al-Qahtani, S. B. A. (2009). *Supplications and treatment with Ruqyah from the Quran and the Sunnah*. Riyadh, Saudi Arabia: Darussalam.

Ameen, A. M. K. (2005). *The jinn and human sickness: Remedies in light of the Quraan and Sunnah*. Translated by Nassiruddin Al-Khattab. Riyadh, Saudi Arabia: Darusalaam.

Basit, A., & Hamid, M. (2010). Mental health issues of Muslim Americans. *Journal of the Islāmic Medical Association of North America*, 42(3), 106–110.

Bukhari (a) *Sahih al-Bukhari 52*. In-book reference: Book 2, Hadith 45. USC-MSA (English) reference: Vol. 1, Book 2, Hadith 50.

Bukhari (b). *Sahih al-Bukhari 3336*. In-book reference: Book 60, Hadith 11. USC-MSA (English) reference: Vol. 1, Book 55, Hadith 552.

Begum, M. (2016). *Can jinn possession and mental illness be the same thing?* http://inspiritedminds.org.uk/2016/10/21can-jinn-possession-and-mental-illness-be-the-same-thing-/ (accessed 30 June 2023).

Himle, J. A., Chatters, L. M., Taylor, R. J., & Nguyen, A. (2011). The relationship between obsessive-compulsive disorder and religious faith: Clinical characteristics and implications for treatment.

Ibn Qayyim, Al-Jawziyyah (1996). *Zaad al-Ma'ad fi Hadyi Khairi al-'Ibad [Provisions for the hereafter in the guidance of the best of servants]*. Riyadh, Saudi Arabia: Dar al-Watan lil-Nashr wa'l-Tawzee'.

Khalifa, N., & Hardie, T. (2005). Possession and jinn. *Journal of the Royal Society of Medicine*, 98(8), 351–353. 10.1177/014107680509800805

Littlewood, R. (2016). Possession states, Chapter 3. In Jean Sybil La Fontaine (Ed.), *The devils children: From spirit possession to witchcraft: New allegations that affect children*. Abingdon, OX: Routledge.

Lim, A., Hoek, H. W., & Blom, J. D. (2015). The attribution of psychotic symptoms to Jinn in Islāmic patients. *Transcultural Psychiatry*, 52(1), 18–32. 10.1177/1363461514543146

Lim, A., Hoek, H. W., Ghane, S., Deen, M., & Blom, J. D. (2018). The attribution of mental health problems to jinn: An explorative study in a transcultural psychiatric outpatient clinic. *Frontiers in Psychiatry*, 9, 89. 10.3389/fpsyt.2018.00089

Muhammad Tim Humble. (n.d.). Muhammad Tim Humble - muhammadtim.com. Retrieved on 12 March 2023 from https://muhammadtim.com/

Nadeer, A. (2021). *The Ruqya handbook: A Practical guide to spiritual healing* (1st ed.). London UK: Al Ruqya Healing.

Rahman, H. A., Hussin, S., & Ridzwan, Z. (2021). Diagnosis of jinn possession amongst patients with mental disorders using thermal imaging. *Sains Insani*, 6(3), 103–106.

Rakesh, K., Arvind, S., Dutt, B. P., Mamta, B., Bhavneesh, S., Kavita, M., Navneet, K., Shrutika, G., Priyanka, B., Arun, K., Harkamal, K., & Jagdeep, K. (2021). The role of religiosity and guilt in symptomatology and outcome of obsessive-compulsive disorder. *Psychopharmacology Bulletin*, 51(3), 38–49.

Rumaysah, A. (Trans.). (2003). *The hearts and their cures*. Birmingham, UK: Darussalam. (Original work published in Arabic, Ibn Taymiyyah, T. al-Qawl al-Mufid 'ala al-Adl wa al-Tawhid).

Rassool, G. Hussein. (2019). *Evil eye, jinn possession, and mental health issues: An Islāmic perspective* (1st ed.). London: Routledge. 10.4324/9781315623764

Shaikh, S., Jones, N., & Farina, F. R. (2019). Islāmic spirituality: A foundation for well-being and resilience. *Journal of Spirituality in Mental Health*, 21(1), 1–20. 10.1080/19349637.2017.1416981

Yorulmaz, O., Gençöz, T., & Woody, S. (2009). OCD cognitions and symptoms in different religious contexts. *Journal of Anxiety Disorders*, 23(3), 401–406.

3 Religious coping from an Islāmic perspective

Introduction

Chapter 3 provides readers with a concise introduction to coping strategies, encompassing both general approaches and those specific to an Islāmic perspective. The aim is to equip readers with an understanding of coping skills and their utilisation within an Islāmic context. Additionally, the chapter explores various Islāmic-based strategies that Muslims employ when faced with challenges and difficulties in their lives, spanning physical, spiritual, and emotional realms. The chapter delves into the healing aspects found in the Qur'ân and *Sunnah*, elucidating how these Islāmic scriptures provide guidance and solace during times of trials and tribulations. Furthermore, it elucidates the concept of well-being from an Islāmic standpoint, highlighting the holistic nature of Islāmic teachings and their impact on individual well-being.

DOI: 10.4324/9781003344827-3

Coping skills

Coping effectively encompasses a broad range of concepts that cover various strategies and behaviours individuals employ to navigate stressful situations and address associated emotional challenges (Lazurus, 1993; Lazaruz & Folkman, 1984). Coping skills are instrumental in shaping how individuals' approach and manage stress, and they play a pivotal role in determining the effectiveness of their coping strategies (Achour et al., 2017). These skills encompass both cognitive and behavioural techniques that individuals employ when confronted with social, emotional, or physical pressures, challenges, and conflicts. This indicates that coping, in its entirety, encompasses a collection of techniques individuals utilise to tackle stressful situations and events, with the aim of reducing stress levels and effectively managing negative emotional responses (Achour et al., 2017).

Religious coping from an Islāmic perspective

Islāmic coping strategies are deeply rooted in Islāmic spirituality and interconnected with different forms of worship and moral discipline (Hermansen, 2005). According to Achour et al. (2017), Islām provides strategies for Muslims to cope with the various challenges and problems that arise in life. These strategies translate Muslims' cognitive perceptions into behavioural patterns while being firmly grounded in their religious emotions. The following Qur'ânic verse addresses the concept of trust.

قُل لَّن يُصِيبَنَا إِلَّا مَا كَتَبَ ٱللَّهُ لَنَا هُوَ مَوْلَىٰنَا وَعَلَى ٱللَّهِ فَلْيَتَوَكَّلِ ٱلْمُؤْمِنُونَ

- *Say, "Never will we be struck except by what God has decreed for us; He is our protector. And upon God let the believers rely."* (Tawbah 9:51, interpretation of the meaning)

During times of adversity, Achour et al. (2017) highlight that reliance on God (*tawakul*) becomes an internal religious coping skill that aids in managing stress, and this approach involves recognising that God never forsakes those who place their trust in Him. Such comforting mechanisms are deeply ingrained and commonly practiced in the religious and socio-cultural lives of Muslims. Muslims frequently hear repeated phrases such as trust in your Lord (*tawakkul 'ala Allāh*), Allāh knows best, or Allāh is great, among others. Achour et al. (2017) further mention that these words hold significant power, reinforcing and providing psychological strength to individuals while acknowledging the supremacy of God in all aspects of life. This resilience is a dynamic process characterised by positive outcomes despite adversity or stress (Luthar et al., 2015). Furthermore, they emphasise God's capability to bring about improvement in the present and future and prevent Muslims from descending into repetitive cycles of apprehension and anxiety about uncertain outcomes. Mujahid (2006) has outlined various approaches employed by Muslims to cope with difficulties and challenges. When a Muslim engages in worship, acknowledging their vulnerabilities and absolute dependence on their Creator, they gain a deeper understanding of the true meaning of the world. This understanding prompts individuals to reflect on their actions, rectify their mistakes, and strive for improvement (Mujahid, 2006).

Islāmic practices such as prayer and supplication to God, patience, trust in God, and recitation of the Qur'ân have the potential to alleviate life stress, depression, and anxiety. These practices draw strength from specific Qur'ânic verses such as those mentioned below that exemplify significant methods for engaging with and resolving difficulties (Achour et al., 2017). Alláh says in the Qur'ân:

وَلِلَّهِ غَيْبُ ٱلسَّمَٰوَٰتِ وَٱلْأَرْضِ وَإِلَيْهِ يُرْجَعُ ٱلْأَمْرُ كُلُّهُ فَٱعْبُدْهُ وَتَوَكَّلْ عَلَيْهِ وَمَا رَبُّكَ بِغَٰفِلٍ عَمَّا تَعْمَلُونَ

- *And to God belong the unseen [aspects] of the heavens and the earth and to Him will be returned the matter, all of it, so worship Him and rely upon Him. And your Lord is not unaware of that which you do.* (Hud 11:123, interpretation of the meaning)

إِنَّ ٱلَّذِينَ قَالُواْ رَبُّنَا ٱللَّهُ ثُمَّ ٱسْتَقَٰمُواْ تَتَنَزَّلُ عَلَيْهِمُ ٱلْمَلَٰئِكَةُ أَلَّا تَخَافُواْ وَلَا تَحْزَنُواْ وَأَبْشِرُواْ بِٱلْجَنَّةِ ٱلَّتِي كُنتُمْ تُوعَدُونَ

- *Indeed, those who have said, "Our Lord is God" and then remained on a right course – the angels will descend upon them, [saying], "Do not fear and do not grieve but receive good tidings of Paradise, which you were promised."* (Fussilat 41:30, interpretation of the meaning)

The notable distinction between Islāmic coping mechanisms and other general coping techniques lies in the significant emphasis placed on the individual's connection with their Creator and their reliance on Him. Muslims come to the realisation that personal power or individual efforts alone do not bring about change or resolve the challenges they encounter. Instead, they understand that positive outcomes arise from their trust in their Lord (Loots, 2008). Moreover, Muslims are effectively guided to follow the example of Prophet Muhammad (ﷺ) in how he navigated stress, managed life's difficulties, and resolved problems. Prophet Muhammad (ﷺ) is reported to have provided guidance to Muslims on adopting religious remedies to cope with grief, anxiety, worry, and fear, which are contributing factors to stress (Loots, 2008; Achour et al., 2017; Karim, 1984). For instance, he encouraged Muslims to engage in the recitation of the Qur'ân, particularly focusing on certain chapters such as chapters 113–114. These chapters urge believers to seek refuge in Almighty God and seek His protection. According to Karim (1984), these practices serve as established anchors in the contemporary treatment of neurosis, which stems from feelings of insecurity and helplessness.

A critical part of religious coping among Muslims is seeking the pleasure of God in all they do with the sincerest of intentions. This must be done for the sake of God alone and seek to acquire His pleasure and avoid His wrath (Mujahid, 2006). It was narrated that Jabir bin Abdullah said, "When the Prophet (☻) started to pray, he would say Alláh is the Greatest (*takbir*), then say,

"Indeed, my prayer (*salah*), my sacrifice, my living, and my dying are for Alláh, the Lord of all that exists. He has no partner. And of this I have been commanded, and I am one of the Muslims. O Alláh, guide me to the best of deeds and the best of manners, for none can guide me to the best of them but You. And protect me from bad deeds and bad manners, for none can protect against them but You" (An Nasa'i (a)).

Mujahid (2006) states that the belief in the hereafter holds significant importance for Muslims and influences their coping strategies in the face of change. Muslims should recognise that they have no authority over the outcomes of events, even when they fulfil their obligations to the best of their abilities. Regardless of the results, Muslims are rewarded for their efforts. An illustration of this is, for instance, upon receiving news of someone's death, Muslims are required to recite the following phrase (interpretation of the meaning): "Surely we belong to God and unto Him shall we return." These words establish a sense of connection with their Lord, an acceptance of His decree, as well as the reality that life is beyond their control, and ultimately, everyone will return to their Creator (Mujahid, 2006; Achour et al., 2017). Al-Munajjid (2006) suggests that while Muslims are promised great rewards in the hereafter, the remembrance of death serves as an opportunity for reflection and consideration of coping approaches in life. It also entails re-evaluating perspectives and dealing with life events and problems in a more optimistic manner.

Different Islāmic coping strategies

Highlighted below are five specific and identifiable Islāmic coping strategies that are commonly used by Muslims during times of adversity, difficulty, and hardship.

Remembrance of God

Mujahid (2006) mentions, for Muslims, the remembrance of God (*dhikr* – referring to all forms of remembrance of God), supplications (*dua'hs*), and recitation of the Qur'ân help them better cope with life problems such as stress and anxiety and also help with psychological and spiritual distress. In feeling the pressures of the heart and burdens of life, Muslims are required to connect to God and indulge themselves in the remembrance of God. Remembrance of God not only implies communicating with One who hears and knows all but also creates a reassuring self-consciousness of a higher authority that can change negative situations and grants patience for overcoming difficulties (Mujahid, 2006). The following Qur'ânic verses highlight the importance of this remembrance:

فَٱذْكُرُونِيَ أَذْكُرْكُمْ وَٱشْكُرُواْ لِي وَلَا تَكْفُرُون

- *So, remember Me; I will remember you. And be grateful to Me and do not deny Me.* (Al-Baqarah 2:152, interpretation of the meaning)

ٱلَّذِينَ ءَامَنُواْ وَتَطْمَئِنُّ قُلُوبُهُم بِذِكْرِ ٱللَّهِّ أَلَا بِذِكْرِ ٱللَّهِ تَطْمَئِنُّ ٱلْقُلُوب

- *Those who have believed and whose hearts are assured by the remembrance of God. Unquestionably, by the remembrance of God hearts are assured.* (Al-Rad 13:28, interpretation of the meaning)

The recitation of the Qur'ân is recognised for its ability to provide solace and peace to the hearts and minds of individuals (Najm, 2015). Recent studies have demonstrated the impact of listening to the recitation of the Qur'ân on human physiological conditions, including the improvement of abnormal heart rates, unhealthy blood pressure, and muscle tension (Achour et al., 2017), and these studies have reported positive outcomes in all cases. In a later chapter of the book, a case study will be presented to further illustrate this point. During challenging times and in the face of illnesses, including mental health conditions (Hermensen, 2005), the recitation of the Qur'ân is utilised as a remedy to seek solace and support. According to Najm (2015), a survey conducted on patients revealed that those who studied the Qur'ân gained increased strength and courage to combat their diseases and found comfort in it. Even individuals with life-threatening conditions reported that reciting the Qur'ân during their prayers brought them a sense of solace. The recitation of the Qur'ân creates a mindset conducive to both psychological and physical healing (Yucel, 2011). Johnsdotter et al. (2011) conducted individual interviews between the period of 2007–2009 among the Somali community living in Sweden. Most of the Somali participants stated that, according to their cultural tradition, Qur'ân recitation was considered the primary and most effective treatment for mental illnesses. They mentioned a practice where they recite Qur'ânic verses and then blow into water, believing that the water becomes infused with healing properties for mental illnesses. This topic will be discussed in greater detail in the chapter on healing from the Qur'ân and *Sunnah* (*ruqyah ash-Shar'iah*).

Remembering God by expressing gratitude and showing appreciation is a prevalent practice among Muslims as a form of religious coping. This spiritual and moral attitude of gratitude is viewed as a highly effective strategy for managing emotional stress (Najm, 2015; Johnsdotter et al., 2011). It not only involves recognising the numerous blessings in one's life but also serves as a motivation for Muslims to be grateful and thankful for what they already possess (Najm, 2015). In a systematic scoping review on the interventions using the Qur'ân to promote mental health, the findings from a study by Owens et al. (2023) showed that prayer, supplications, recitation, reading, memorising, and listening to the Qur'ân reduce anxiety, depression, and stress and increase quality of life and coping.

Importance of prayer

Prayer (*salah*) is a commonly utilised religious strategy among Muslims to cope with hardships in their lives. It serves to cultivate a heightened awareness of the divine presence and fulfils the spiritual need for a connection with the Creator, providing solace and comfort to the soul (Karim, 1984). From a mental health perspective, *salah*, which necessitates reliance on the Creator, plays a role in the prevention and treatment of various neuroses and even major psychological disorders (Karim, 1984). During the preparatory stage of prayer, Muslims are encouraged to shift their focus away from the material aspects of the world, including their burdens and worries. However, during the act of prayer, Muslims experience a profound connection with God, from whom they derive maximum support (Tala'at, 2006). According to Karim (1984), regular prayer serves as a continuous psychological and emotional catalyst for Muslims. It enables them to effectively navigate the changes in their surroundings and make decisions aligned with the essence of prayer and their evolving connection with God.

Forgiveness and fortitude

Achour et al. (2017) discuss the three terms used in the Qur'ân to describe forgiveness: *afw, safh, and ghafara.* Prophet Muhammed (ﷺ) taught Muslims the practice of forgiveness for various reasons, including calming oneself, reducing anxiety and worries, and alleviating depression. An example that highlights this point is the following tradition: "If anyone continually asks pardon, God Almighty will provide for him a way out of every distress, and a relief from every anxiety, and will appoint for him from where he did not reckon" (Tabarani, 1995).

In Islām, forgiveness is viewed from two perspectives: forgiveness from God and forgiveness among humans. Just as it is essential to believe in God's mercy and forgiveness, it is also necessary to base human relationships on forgiveness. Refusing to forgive others' mistakes will not provide a solution for the current problems. Instead, it will only exacerbate the issues, leading to potential consequences for both physical and psychological well-being (Ross et al., 2017). Numerous theories have made a clear distinction between forgiveness and reconciliation, with the most recent concept emphasising the restoration of relationships between wrongdoers and victims (Warsah, 2020). According to the holistic definitions of forgiveness, it is possible to forgive a harmful offender while also achieving a state of peace. The capacity for humans to forgive others stems from the ancestral responsibility of our predecessors to enhance strategies and reap the benefits of repairing relationships (McCullough et al., 2013). Through an Islāmic lens, it is incumbent upon Muslims to forgive others, even their enemies, as it is one of the most important teachings (Achour et al., 2007). In the Qur'ân, God has described the believers as:

وَٱلَّذِينَ يَجْتَنِبُونَ كَبَٰئِرَ ٱلْإِثْمِ وَٱلْفَوَٰحِشَ وَإِذَا مَا غَضِبُوا۟ هُمْ يَغْفِرُونَ

- *Those who avoid major sins and acts of indecencies and when they are angry they forgive.* (As-Shura 42:37, interpretation of the meaning)

In Islām, fortitude is regarded as one of the best spiritual and moral characteristics. The Qur'ân sees fortitude as significant for success (Al-Imran 3:200). The Qur'ân also promises Muslims with a great recompense which encompasses blessings, mercy, and guidance (Al-Baqarah 2:155–157). For example, Allāh states in the Qur'ân:

ٱلَّذِينَ يُنفِقُونَ فِي ٱلسَّرَّاءِ وَٱلضَّرَّاءِ وَٱلْكَٰظِمِينَ ٱلْغَيْظَ وَٱلْعَافِينَ عَنِ ٱلنَّاسِ وَٱللَّهُ يُحِبُّ ٱلْمُحْسِنِينَ

- *Who spend [in the cause of God] during ease and hardship and who restrain anger and who pardon the people – and God loves the doers of good.* (Al-Imran, 3:134, interpretation of the meaning)

The term patience (*sabr*) and its derivatives are mentioned more than 70 times in the Qur'ân. The importance of this number can be understood in light of the fact that Islām compensates Muslims for good acts, from 10-fold to 700-fold, with exception to someone who bears in patience, his reward then being immeasurable (Ibn Hibban, 1993). Allāh mentions in chapter two of the Qur'ân, where focus is drawn on the concept of patience and the reality and acceptance that Allāh shall test people's patience in many ways.

God Almighty said:

وَلَنَبْلُوَنَّكُم بِشَيْءٍ مِّنَ ٱلْخَوْفِ وَٱلْجُوعِ وَنَقْصٍ مِّنَ ٱلْأَمْوَٰلِ وَٱلْأَنفُسِ وَٱلثَّمَرَٰتِ ۗ وَبَشِّرِ ٱلصَّٰبِرِينَ

- *We will certainly test you with something of fear and hunger, and loss of wealth and lives and fruits (earnings); but give glad tidings to the persevering and patient.* (Al-Baqarah 2: 155, interpretation of the meaning)

These concepts are reinforced by various religious traditions, as exemplified by the following saying: "Wonderous are the believer's affairs. For him, there is good in all his affairs, and this is true only for the believer. When something pleasing happens to him, he is grateful, and that is good for him. And when something displeasing happens to him, he exercises patience (sabr), and that is good for him" (Ibn Hibban, cited in Achour et al., 2017). Muslims believe that ease and comfort generally parallel hardship and difficulties, as Alláh has mentioned,

فَإِنَّ مَعَ ٱلْعُسْرِ يُسْرًا

- *For indeed with hardship will be ease.* (As-Sharh 94:5, interpretation of the meaning)

and as such, Muslims gather their strength and energy to reach the stage following patience.

Within the Islāmic faith, great significance is attributed to the extent and nature of patience exhibited during the initial response to life's difficulties or tests, known as ibtila (Achour et al., 2017). Prophet Muhammad (ﷺ) is reported to have emphasised the importance of patience by stating, "Verily, patience is at the first stroke of a calamity" (Bukhari (a)). These tests are also regarded as opportunities for personal growth, as they can contribute to the strengthening of one's character, emotional resilience, and purification of the soul.

Collective communal support

The heterogenous Muslim community, encompassing relatives, friends, and extended members, plays a significant role in providing collective moral support. This support takes various forms, including emotional, spiritual, religious, and even financial assistance, as the community shares a moral responsibility to aid and uplift one another (Mundhiri, 2000). This emotional and religious sense of belonging fosters effective coping strategies among Muslims in the face of calamities, tests, and challenges. In providing emotional support by consoling others and offering genuine advice and guidance, it is important to note that these layers of support respect people's privacy, personal space, and moments of solitude. They serve as a means to foster individual growth and contribute to the development of a healthy community (Achour et al., 2017).

It is in this context that we understand the instruction of Prophet Muhammad (ﷺ): "There are not three people, either in the town or in the desert, among whom prayer is not said in congregation but the devil will surely overcome them; so, stick to the congregation for the wolf eats the one that has strayed away from the flock" (An Nasa'i (b)). Hence, it is imperative for Muslims to share and be of benefit to their fellow brothers and sisters in Islām and to be in the service of others (Mundhiri, 2000). Enduring life's challenges and negative circumstances becomes more manageable when individuals have strong emotional and religious connections within their community. This contributes to an improved ability to cope with stress (Achour et al., 2017). The findings from research suggest that the preservation of Muslims' mental health has been recognised as dependent on the crucial aspect of maintaining social support through affiliation with religious communities (Wang et al., 2020; Basit & Hamid, 2010). In addition, the findings further indicate that active participation in religious activities and regular attendance at mosques play a pivotal role in facilitating the recovery of Muslims from mental illnesses. Furthermore, such engagement has been linked to a reduction in depression rates and an enhancement in social functioning (Eltaiba & Harries, 2015; Abdel-Khalek, 2007).

Islāmic cognitive behavioural therapy (CBT) or positive thinking

Muslims employ this coping strategy remarkably to navigate and manage life's challenges and struggles. This approach is rooted in their belief in God and is

sustained through their dedicated spiritual engagement (Machouche et al., 2012). Such constructive
thinking fosters an optimistic outlook regarding emotional and physiological adjustments in individuals'
lives, enabling them to cultivate gratitude and preventing negative emotions such as despondency,
sadness, and hopelessness. Furthermore, positive
thinking is closely tied to a Muslim's belief in the
Almighty God. An integral aspect of this is the
expectation of goodness from God. God conscious-
ness profoundly influences the awareness, emotions,
and behavioral and social interactions of Muslims
(Machouche et al., 2012). As highlighted by Achour
et al. (2017), various life events, such as birth or death,
prosperity or poverty, health or sickness, marriage or
divorce, friendship or loneliness, isolation or interaction, rise or decline, serve as real testing grounds for
the power of positive thinking. These occurrences not
only test individuals but also provide opportunities for
the development of positive thinking skills
(Machouche et al., 2012). Allāh states in the Qur'ān:

كُتِبَ عَلَيْكُمُ ٱلْقِتَالُ وَهُوَ كُرْهٌ لَّكُمْ وَعَسَىٰٓ أَن تَكْرَهُواْ شَيْئًا وَهُوَ خَيْرٌ لَّكُمْ
وَعَسَىٰٓ أَن تُحِبُّواْ شَيْئًا وَهُوَ شَرٌّ لَّكُمْ وَٱللَّهُ يَعْلَمُ وَأَنتُمْ لَا تَعْلَمُونَ

- *But perhaps you hate a thing and it is good for*
  you; and perhaps you love a thing and it is bad for
  you. And God knows, while you know not. (Al-
  Baqarah 2: 216, interpretation of the meaning)

The outcome of this kind of thinking in relation to
the process of coping with trials and tests is that it

enables people to develop a sense of resilience, hopefulness, and comfort and prevents excessive worry, reluctance, and fear (Machouche et al., 2012; Hermensen, 2005). The strategies mentioned above are not presented in a particular order of preference and can be adapted as needed. They exemplify the resilience that Muslims possess in coping with the various life stressors that they encounter.

Healing from the Qur'ân and *Sunnah*

In Muslim communities, it is observed that people often combine traditional medical treatments and spiritual remedies in their pursuit of healing (Yucel, 2011). Scholars who consider the Qur'ân as a source of healing rely on specific verses on healing (*shifa*) and a narrative from the Prophet's life recounted by Abu Said Al-Khudri. According to the narration, a group of the Prophet's companions encountered an inhospitable tribe of Arabs. While in their company, the chief of that tribe was bitten by a snake or stung by a scorpion. The companions were asked if they had any medicine or someone who could perform spiritual healing (*ruqyah*). The companions responded that they would not treat the chief unless they were compensated. The tribe agreed to offer a flock of sheep in exchange. One of the companions then recited the opening chapter (*Surah-al-Fatiha*), collected his saliva, and applied it to the bite. As a result, the patient was cured, and the tribe presented the sheep as promised. However, the companions insisted on consulting the Prophet (ﷺ) about accepting the sheep. Upon being asked, the Prophet (ﷺ) smiled and confirmed the legitimacy of Surah-al-Fatiha as a form of *ruqyah*. He allowed them to accept the sheep and requested a share for himself (Bukhari (b)).

The Prophet (ﷺ) emphasised that healing should align with the teachings of the Qur'ân. Moreover, Prophet Muhammad (ﷺ) himself supplicated for the well-being of the sick, including those who were mentally and spiritually afflicted. In the Qur'ân, Allāh instructs Muslims to follow the *Sunnah*, as Prophet Muhammad (ﷺ) serves as the ultimate role model (Sered & Barnes, 2005). The extensive collection of Prophetic sayings (*hadīth*) covering areas such as medicine, prayer, and health has given rise to the field of Prophetic medicine (*tibb- an- nabawi*). These *hadīth* encompass both remedies and preventive measures (Sered & Barnes, 2005). Imam Bukhari, a prominent source of Prophetic sayings, directly narrated numerous *hadīths* pertaining to medicine, prayer, and healing. He compiled two books specifically dedicated to physical and spiritual healing (Al-Suyuti,1962).

According to Yucel's research (2011), Muslim scholars have highlighted the comprehensive nature of healing, which encompasses physical, psychological, and spiritual aspects. They assert that in order to overcome illness, individuals should pursue both physical treatments and spiritual fortification. The various forms of worship in Islām, such *as salah, dua'hs,* recitation of the Qur'ân, and remembrance of Allāh, contribute to the development of a mindset that promotes spiritual healing, overall well-being, as well as physical recovery, alleviation of suffering, and the ability to overcome illness (Yucel, 2011).

Well-being in the Islāmic context

According to Islāmi (2003), in Islām, the attainment of well-being is achieved through adherence to the Islāmic law (*Shar'iah*), while engaging in sinful actions leads to ill-being. Even those individuals who strive to follow the righteous path often encounter internal temptations and negative forces that push them towards wrongdoing and transgressions. This inherent contradiction necessitates a continuous struggle to overcome these forces. In Islām, this ongoing battle is referred to as "the major jihad," representing the primary internal struggle that humans face. Muslims are encouraged to actively partake in this internal battle, continuously striving to obey Alláh's commands (Islāmi, 2003). According to Joshanloo and Weijers (2019), the Qur'ân portrays the worldly life as transient and filled with allure, often described as "play and amusement" (Al-Anam 6:32). However, the materialistic nature of this world can hinder the attainment of true well-being, as it diverts individuals from remembering Alláh. Consequently, one may forfeit the everlasting pleasures and goodness of the hereafter (Al Munafiqoon 63:9 and Al-Ala 87:17).

Furthermore, life in this world is inherently characterised by inevitable suffering and hardship, making it impossible for a person to achieve complete and genuine happiness solely within worldly confines. It is important to acknowledge that while the focus in Islām is primarily on well-being in the hereafter, some degree of well-being can be attained in this world (Joshanloo & Weijers, 2019). The ideal well-being in this world entails unwavering devotion to Allāh, adherence to the *Shar'iah*, cultivating a strong personal relationship with Allāh, and securing one's happiness in the afterlife, which is accompanied by a sense of reassurance bestowed by Allāh. Therefore, from a Muslim perspective, one's life in the material world can still be deemed good and valuable, as Muslims are encouraged to pray and seek goodness in both this world and the hereafter. However, the absolute and genuine version of well-being is not fully achievable within the confines of this world (Joshanloo, 2013).

One of the purposes of human existence in this world, in addition to worshiping Allāh and seeking His pleasure, is to serve as a test to determine whether individuals are worthy of true well-being in the hereafter. As Muslims, our faith (*Iman*) is continuously tested in this worldly life through both blessings and hardships (Joshanloo, 2013; Joshanloo & Weijers, 2019).

ٱلَّذِي خَلَقَ ٱلْمَوْتَ وَٱلْحَيَوٰةَ لِيَبْلُوَكُمْ أَيُّكُمْ أَحْسَنُ عَمَلاً وَهُوَ ٱلْعَزِيزُ ٱلْغَفُورُ

- *[He] who created death and life to test you [as to] which of you is best in deed – and He is the Exalted in Might, the Forgiving.* (Al-Mulk, 67:2, interpretation of the meaning)

The trials and hardships that Muslims experience serve as a test of their belief in Allāh's profound knowledge and wisdom. These difficulties allow them to assess whether they can accept the hardships as part of Allāh's grand plan and whether such challenges bring them closer to Allāh (Joshansloo, 2013). On the other hand, the blessings bestowed upon Muslims also serve as a test. They examine whether Muslims genuinely understand their purpose on earth, which is to serve and worship Allāh, regardless of life's circumstances. Sometimes, when people receive blessings, they may become preoccupied with pursuing worldly possessions without acknowledging that all success is granted by Allāh (Achour et al., 2017). This may lead to ingratitude towards Allāh or a failure to utilise their blessings to help those in need. These ongoing tests reflect the depth of a Muslim's faith and determine the extent to which they will strive to achieve ultimate well-being in the hereafter (Joshanloo & Weijers, 2019).

Before concluding this section, it is important to discuss the role of human reason and intellect in relation to well-being within the Islāmic framework. Abu-Raiya's (2012) in-depth analysis of Qur'ânic verses suggests that the primary function of human intellect in Islām is to contemplate the revelations and Allāh, as well as to control and discipline one's negative inclinations. Therefore, human reason and intellect, when detached from religious principles, cannot serve as an autonomous means to achieve well-being. In other words, well-being cannot be attained solely through rationality; rather, rationality is merely one of many tools that can assist individuals in their submission and devotion to Alláh (Johanson & Weijers, 2019). Alláh knows best.

References

Abu-Raiya, H. (2012). Towards a systematic Qura'nic theory of personality. *Mental Health, Religion & Culture*, 15(3), 217–233.

Abdel-Khalek, A. M. (2007). Religiosity, happiness, health, and psychopathology in a probability sample of Muslim adolescents. *Mental Health, Religion & Culture*, 10(6), 571–583. 10.1080/13674670601034547

Al-Munajjid, M. S. (2006). *Dealing with worries and stress.* http://www.Islām-qa.com/index.php?Pgarticle& lneng&article

Al-Suyuti, J. A. (1962). *Tibb-ul Nabbi (Medicine of the Prophet).* (C. Elgood, Trans.). London: Ta-Ha Publishers.

Achour, M., Bensaid, B., & Mohd Nor, M. R. (2017). An Islāmic perspective on coping with life stressors. Applied research in quality of life. *The Official Journal of the International Society for Quality-of-Life Studies*: Springer.

An- Nasa'i (a). *Sunan an-Nasa'i* 896. In book reference: Book 11, Hadith 21, English translation: Vol. 2, Book 11, Hadith 897.

An- Nasa'i (b). *Sunan an-Nasa'i* 847. In book reference: Book 10, Hadith 71, English translation: Vol. 1, Book 10, Hadith 848.

Basit, A., & Hamid, M. (2010). Mental health issues of Muslim Americans. *Journal of the Islamic Medical Association of North America*, 42(3). doi:106-10:10.5915/ 42-3-5507

Bukhari (a). *Sahih al-Bukhari* 1302. In-book reference: Book 23, Hadith 60. USC-MSA (English) reference: Vol. 2, Book 23, Hadith 389.

Bukhari (b). *Sahih al-Bukhari* 5736. In-book reference: Book 76, Hadith 51. USC-MSA (English) reference: Vol. 7, Book 71, Hadith 632.

Eltaiba, N., & Harries, M. (2015). Reflections on recovery in mental health: Perspectives from a Muslim culture. *Social Work in Health Care*, 54(8), 725–737.

Hermansen, M. (2005). Dimensions of Islāmic religious healing. In D. G. Hufford (Ed.), *Religion and healing in America* (pp. 407–422). New York, NY: Oxford University Press.

Ibn Hibban. (1993). *Sahih Ibn Hibban bi-Tartib Ibn Bilban*. (S. al-Arna'ut, Ed. 2). Beirut: Mu'assassat al-Risalah.

Islāmi, S. H. (2003). *Imam Khomeini: Ethics and politics*. (M. Limba, Trans.). Tehran, Iran: The Institute for Compilation and Publication of Imam Khomeini's Work.

Joshanloo, M. (2013). A comparison of Western and Islāmic conceptions of happiness. *Journal of Happiness Studies*, 14(6), 1857–1874.

Joshanloo, M., & Weijers, D. (2019). Islāmic perspectives on wellbeing. In F. A. Abubakar, D. Weijers, & M. Joshanloo (Eds.), *Positive psychology in the Middle East/North Africa* (pp. 237–256). doi:10.1007/978-3-030-13921-6_11.

Johnsdotter, S., Ingvarsdotter, K., Östman, M., & Carlbom, A. (2011). Koran reading and negotiation with jinn: Strategies to deal with mental ill health among Swedish Somalis. *Mental Health, Religion & Culture*, 14(8), 741–755.

Karim, G. M. (1984). *Islāmization of psychology. Third international seminar on Islāmic thought. Malaysia*: Kuala Lumpur.

Lazarus, R. S. (1993) Coping theory and research: Past, present, and future. *Psychometric Medicine*, 55, 234–247.

Lazarus, R. S., & Folkman, S. (1984). *Stress, appraisal, and coping.* New York: Springer.

Loots, S. (2008). *The role of exposure to suicide and coping strategies in the suicidal ideation of adolescents.* Bloemfontein: University of the Free State.

Luthar, S. S., Crossman, E. J., & Small, P. J. (2015). Resilience and adversity. In M. E., lamb & R. M., Learner (Eds.), *Handbook of child psychology and developmental science: Socioemotional processes* (pp. 247–286). John Wiley&Sons, Inc.

Machouche, S., Bensaid, B., & Grine, F. (2012). Positive thinking: An Islāmic perspective. Al-Shajarah: *Journal of the International Institute of Islāmic Thought and Civilization (ISTAC)*, 17(2), 225–256.

McCullough, M. E., Kurzban, R., & Tabak, B. A. (2013). Cognitive systems for revenge and forgiveness. *Behavioral and Brain Sciences*, 36(1), 1–15. 10.1017/ S0140525X11002160

Mujahid, A. M. (2006). *25 ways to deal with stress and anxiety.* www.soundvision.com/info/peace/stresstips.asp (accessed 12 July 2023).

Mundhiri, A. (2000). *Al-Targhib wal-Tarhib, Ed. Muhammad al-Sayyed.* Cairo: Dar al-Fajr lil-Turath, Ed. 1, Vol. 3: 323.

Najm, S. (2015). *Impact of Islāmic practices on the mental health of Muslims.* https://www.academia.edu/20811677/

Owens, J., Rassool, G. Hussein, Bernstein, J., Latif, S., & Aboul-Enein, B., (2023). Interventions using the Qur'an to promote mental health: A systematic scoping review. *Journal of Mental Health.* https://www.tandf online.com/doi/full/10.1080/09638237.2023.2232449

Ross, R. W. J., Boon, S. D., & Stackhouse, M. R. D. (2017). Redefining unforgiveness: Exploring victims' experiences in the wake of unforgiven interpersonal transgressions. *Deviant Behavior*, 1–13. 10.1080/01639625.2017. 1399747

Sered, S. S., & Barnes, L. L. (2005). Introduction. In S., Sered & L., Barnes (Eds.), *Religion and healing in America*(pp. 3–26). New York: Oxford University Press.

Tala'at, M. D. (2006). Islām and stress management (Part 4): Islāmic coping mechanisms. http://theIslāmicworkplace.com/2006/12/23/Islām-and-stress-management-part-4-Islāmic-coping-mechanisms/ (accessed 6 July 2023).

Tabarani, A. S. (1995). *Al-Mu'jam al-Awsat, Ed. Tariq bin 'Awadh & Muhsin al-Husayni*, Cairo: Dar al-Haramayn, Ed. 1, 6, 240.

Wang, S. C., Raja, A. H., & Azhar, S. (2020). 'A lot of us have a very difficult time reconciling what being Muslim is': A phenomenological study on the meaning of being Muslim. *American, Cultural Diversity and Ethnic Minority Psycholgy,* 26(3), 338–346. 10.1037/cdp0000297

Warsah, I. (2020). Forgiveness viewed from positive psychology and Islām. *Islāmic Guidance and Counseling Journal,* 3(2). 10.25217/igcj.v3i2.878

Yücel, S. (2011), *Prayer and healing in Islām with addendum of 25 remedies for the Sick* by Said Nursi. New Jersey: Tughra Books.

4   Adkhaar as a spiritual intervention

Introduction

Islām instructs Muslims to seek refuge and protection in Alláh from various forms of harm, including physical, psychological, and spiritual afflictions such as the evil eye, envy, *jinn* possession, or black magic. This is achieved through reciting specific verses from the Qur'ân, as well as supplications and invocations prescribed by the Prophet (ﷺ) (Nadeer, 2021; Al Qahtani, 2009). The Islāmic belief system emphasises the prevention and treatment of spiritual and other afflictions, rooted in the concepts of Islāmic monotheism (*tawheed*) and trust and reliance on God alone(*tawakkul*) (Nadeer, 2021). The significance of making supplication (*dua'h*) to Alláh is immeasurable. Ibn al-Qayyim Al Jawziyyah states, *dua'h* is one of the most beneficial remedies. It is the enemy of calamity; repelling it, curing it, preventing its occurrence, and alleviating it or reducing it if it befalls anyone. It is the weapon of the believer (Al-Jawziyyah cited in Wyatt, 2020). In this

DOI: 10.4324/9781003344827-4

chapter, we will provide a brief explanation of these key concepts and highlight the importance of the remembrance of Alláh (*adhkaar*) as a spiritual intervention and a means of protection against distress and harm. The benefits and virtues of *adhkaar* will also be explored, illustrating its role as a primary preventative intervention that can be integrated into therapeutic practice.

Tawheed, tawakkul, and *adhkaar*

Tawheed refers to the belief in and worship of Alláh as the sole God and Lord, ascribing all divine attributes exclusively to Him (Islām Q&A, 2010a). *Tawakkul*, on the other hand, is derived from the Arabic expression *tawakkala yatawakkilu-tawakkulan* or *tawak-kulan*, which means to appoint or rely on a counsellor, agent, or representative (Yunus, 1990). This implies that human understanding and practical application are significant in implementing these concepts in everyday life (Huda et al., 2019).

As pointed out in the Qur'ân:

لَهُ مُعَقِّبَٰتٌ مِّنۢ بَيْنِ يَدَيْهِ وَمِنْ خَلْفِهِۦ يَحْفَظُونَهُۥ مِنْ أَمْرِ ٱللَّهِ إِنَّ ٱللَّهَ لَا يُغَيِّرُ مَا بِقَوْمٍ حَتَّىٰ يُغَيِّرُواْ مَا بِأَنفُسِهِمْ وَإِذَآ أَرَادَ ٱللَّهُ بِقَوْمٍ سُوٓءًا فَلَا مَرَدَّ لَهُۥ وَمَا لَهُم مِّن دُونِهِۦ مِن وَالٍ

- For him [i.e., each one] are successive [angels] before and behind him who protect him by the decree of God. Indeed, God will not change the condition of a people until they change what is in themselves. And when God intends for a

people ill, there is no repelling it. And there is
not for them besides Him any patron. (Al-Ra'd,
13:11, interpretation of the meaning)

Belief in predestination is a fundamental aspect of
the Islāmic faith, included within its six pillars of
belief. This principle implies that individuals should
act in accordance with their abilities while recognising that their destinies are ultimately determined
by Allāh. It encourages proactive engagement rather
than complacency. Regardless of the circumstances,
Muslims are urged to fulfil their responsibilities and
trust in Allāh for the outcomes (Basri, 2008).
Seeking refuge in Allāh provides a profound sense
of security, acting as a psychological shield, as
stated by Qamar (2013). However, for this shield
to be effective, it is essential to adhere to the two
fundamental concepts of *tawheed and tawakkul*
discussed earlier.

The concept of *adhkaar* involves the remembrance
and glorification of Allāh the Almighty, and it is
expressed through various forms. Rassool (2019)
explains that *adhkaar* should be deeply ingrained
in the heart, reflected in one's speech, and demonstrated through righteous actions and deeds. It goes
without saying that *tawheed and tawakkul* serve
as foundational pillars for this process.

Adkhaar as a protection from all forms of distress and harm

Adhkaar can be categorised into two types: general
adhkaar and specific *adhkaar*. General *adhkaar* refers

to the remembrance of Alláh at any time during the day or night, without any limitations or prescribed quantities, as stated by the Prophet (🕋) (Wyatt, 2020). This form of *dhikr* includes reciting the Qur'ân, uttering phrases seeking forgiveness from Alláh, like (*Astaghfirullah*), Glory be to Alláh (Subhan Allah), Praise be to Alláh (*Alhamdulillah*), there is no deity but Alláh (*La ilaha illa Alláh*), Alláh is the Greatest (*Alláhu Akbar*), there is no power or strength except with Alláh (*La hawlawala quwwata illa billah*), and invoking the names of Alláh. Engaging in seeking knowledge, promoting good deeds, and preventing evil actions also falls under the realm of general *adhkaar*, as they involve the remembrance of Alláh (lifewithAlláh.com). On the other hand, specific *adhkaar* are supplications and remembrances that are associated with places or situations, for example, making a supplication (*dua'h*) in the marketplace or during times of distress. These specific *adhkaar* are recited in prescribed quantities and may have specific wordings. They include dua'hs to be recited in the morning and evening, before sleeping, after each of the five daily prayers, and *adhkaar* associated with various everyday actions such as eating, wearing clothes, entering and leaving the bathroom, and entering and leaving the home (Wyatt, 2020; lifewithAlláh.com). In summary, general *adhkaar* encompasses the remembrance of Alláh at any time and in any amount, while specific *adhkaar* are supplications and remembrances tied to specific places, situations, and quantities. Both types of *adhkaar* play a significant role in the spiritual practice of Muslims.

It is crucial to strengthen ourselves by engaging in prescribed daily prayers of remembrance in the morning and evening. It is widely recognised that prevention is better than cure. However, there is often confusion or misconception regarding the terms *adkhaar* and *ruqyah.*

Adkhaar primarily serves as a means of protection and prevention from all kinds of affliction and harm, while *ruqyah* refers to the method of curing existing harm, which is similarly, not limited or restricted to spiritual ailments alone (Nadeer, 2021). Scholars have differed in their opinions regarding the specific start and end times for morning and evening *adkhaar.* Some scholars suggest that the prescribed time for morning *adkhaar* begins at dawn and concludes at sunrise. Others propose that it ends when the forenoon (*al-duha*) ends. However, the preferred time is from the beginning of dawn until the sun has fully risen. As for the evening *adkhaar*, some scholars state that it begins at the time of (*Asr*) prayer and concludes at sunset, while others argue that it extends until one-third of the night has passed. Additionally, some scholars have mentioned that the time for evening *adkhaar* commences after sunset (Ummah Welfare Trust, 2018; Wyatt, 2020).

It is thought that the most appropriate view according to scholars such as Imam An-Nawawi, Ibn-Al-Qayyim Al-Jawziyyah, and Ibn Hajer is that a person should strive to recite the morning *adkhaar* between dawn and sunrise, if he then misses it, it will be acceptable for one to recite them before the time of the forenoon ends, which is shortly before the time for *dhuhr* prayer (lifewithAlláh.com). He should recite the evening *adkhaars* between the time of *Asr* and *Maghrib*, then if he misses this period, he should recite them before one-third of the night has passed. The evidence for this preference is because the Qur'ân urges us to remember Alláh in the early morning and in the late afternoon, which is understood to be the time between *Asr* and *Maghrib* (Islām Q&A, 2010b).

Reciting these prescriptive prayers will not only help Muslims in terms of protection from harm and affliction, but also likely transform their lives in terms of overall well-being, spiritual well-being, a sense of inner peace and tranquillity, and softening of the heart. This is emphasised in the following verses in the Qur'ân:

ٱلَّذِينَ ءَامَنُواْ وَتَطۡمَئِنُّ قُلُوبُهُم بِذِكۡرِ ٱللَّهِ أَلَا بِذِكۡرِ ٱللَّهِ تَطۡمَئِنُّ ٱلۡقُلُوبُ

• Those who have believed and whose hearts are assured by the remembrance of God. Unquestionably, by the remembrance of God hearts are assured. (Ar- Rad 13:28, interpretation of the meaning)

أَفَمَن شَرَحَ ٱللَّهُ صَدۡرَهُۥ لِلۡإِسۡلَٰمِ فَهُوَ عَلَىٰ نُورٍ مِّن رَّبِّهِۦ فَوَيۡلٌ لِّلۡقَٰسِيَةِ قُلُوبُهُم مِّن ذِكۡرِ ٱللَّهِ أُوْلَٰئِكَ فِي ضَلَٰلٍ مُّبِينٍ

• So, is one whose breast God has expanded to [accept] Islām and he is upon i.e., guided by a light from his Lord like one whose heart rejects it? Then woe to those whose hearts are hardened against the remembrance of God. Those are in manifest error. (Az – Zumar: 39:22, interpretation of the meaning)

Benefits and virtues of *adkhaar*

Below are a number of benefits and virtues of *adkhaar* which extend beyond the spiritual realm and encompass all avenues of well-being in the life of a Muslim:

Reaffirming the Oneness of Alláh (*tawheed*) and servitude to Him

Through these prayers, you affirm the oneness *tawheed,* uniqueness, and absolute perfection of Alláh daily, along with acknowledging one's limitations and need of Him, essentially submitting ourselves to Him and realising that this is where our reliance belongs in all aspects of life. The daily adkhaar done consistently will bring us to love Alláh, fear Him, place all our hopes and needs in Him, submit, and give thanks to Him (Nadeer, 2021).

Experience encompasses well-being (*aafiyah*) in this life and the next and earn invaluable rewards

The Prophet (﷽) gave glad tidings of unparalleled reward to those who hold onto the rope of *adhkaar.* Some of these include, sins being forgiven, protection from all harm, protection against anxiety, worries, and distress, salvation from Alláh's anger and wrath, and the harm/evil of mankind and devils.

Other rewards also include entrance into paradise and protection from hellfire (lifewithAlláh.com).

Acquire blessings in your day and feeling a sense of peace and contentment

Ibn Al-Qayyim Al-Jawziyyah states that there are four acts that bring overall sustenance to a person: (1) standing for the night prayer (*qiyam*), (2) plentiful repentance (*istighfar*) before dawn, (3) a commitment to giving regular charity, and (4) *dhikr* in the morning and evening (Ummah Welfare Trust, 2018). Alláh revealed the following verse in the Qur'ân to the Prophet (ﷺ) when he was being persecuted in Makkah:

فَٱصۡبِرۡ عَلَىٰ مَا يَقُولُونَ وَسَبِّحۡ بِحَمۡدِ رَبِّكَ قَبۡلَ طُلُوعِ ٱلشَّمۡسِ وَقَبۡلَ ٱلۡغُرُوبِ

- So be patient, [O Muhammad], over what they say and exalt [God] with praise of your Lord before the rising of the sun and before its setting. (Qaf 50:39, interpretation of the meaning)

This verse teaches us that during times of difficulty, we should hold on to two gems, i.e., patience (*sabr*) and remembering Alláh (*dhikr*) in the morning and the evening. During these times, we are able to observe and reflect on the change that takes place in the universe as the night changes into day, and the day changes into night by the permission of Alláh. Through this conscious engagement with *dhikr* and ponderance, the hearts become calm and reflective, and the troubles of our daily life become less weighty (Ummah Welfare Trust, 2018).

A protection from all types of evil and affliction

One of the most important benefits of being consistent with daily morning and evening *adkhaar* is that it serves as a protection from all forms of evil and harm. This includes and is not limited to illnesses, anxiety, grief, depression, criminals, devils among men and *jinn*, evil eye, and magic (Ummah Welfare Trust, 2018; Nadeer, 2021; Al-Jawziyyah, 2020). Ibn Kathir the well-known Qur'ânic exegete said that one should "wear the coat" of *adhkaar* so it can protect you from the evil of human and jinn alike, and cover your souls with seeking forgiveness, so it can erase the sins of the night and day (Islam Q&A, 2018a). Similarly, Ibn Al Qayyim has mentioned that the morning and evening *adhkaar* function as a shield; the thicker the shield, the more its owner will be protected. In fact, its strength can reach to the extent that the arrow shot at it will bounce back to affect the one who shot it in the first place (productivemuslim.com). The well-known scholar, Sheikh Uthaymeen said, that for the one whose heart is present, the morning and evening *adhkaar* serve as a stronger fortress than the wall of Gog and Magog (*Ya'jooj* and *Ma'jooj*) (productive-muslim.com).

The recommended daily adkhaar

Muslims believe that the Prophet (ﷺ) was the pinnacle of guidance and advice. It is therefore not arguable that the *adhkaar* specifically prescribed by the Prophet (ﷺ) will be the best choice to model.

This can be understood in the example of the *hadīth* regarding his wife Juwayriyah: "Once, the Prophet (ﷺ) returned in the forenoon and asked her if she had continued to remember Alláh in the same position, as he had found her doing so before he left for fajr prayer. When she replied in the affirmative, he told her, "I recited four phrases three times after I left you. If everything that you have said today was put on the scales, this would outweigh it" (Muslim(a)). The words were:

سُبْحَانَ اللّٰهِ وَبِحَمْدِهِ ، عَدَدَ خَلْقِهِ ، وَرِضَا نَفْسِهِ ، وَزِنَةَ عَرْشِهِ ، وَمِدَادَ كَلِمَاتِهِ

Glory is to Alláh and praise is to Him, by the multitude of His creation, by His pleasure, by the weight of His Throne, and by the extent of His words. (Interpretation of the meaning).

The above displays that true wisdom is to follow what is prescribed based on the immense virtue and benefit. This narration further teaches us the concept of quality trumping quantity. Furthermore, the perfection in wording and depth of meaning in the prescribed *adkhaar* remains unparalleled. The Prophet (ﷺ) therefore offers the perfect formulae with guaranteed returns. It is necessary to mention that there are many sound *adkhaar* for the morning and evening and before sleeping that were narrated in the *Sunnah*. Imam An-Nawawi stated, "You should understand that the narrations and reports concerning this matter are many; what we have mentioned is sufficient for the one who is enabled to act upon them. We refrain from quoting more for fear of tiring the student. Moreover, it is better for a person to do all that is mentioned concerning that, but if that is not possible, he should stick to what he is able to do of the most important thereof" (Al-Adhkar, p. 95 cited from (Islām Q&A, 2018b)). Keeping with this view, and for purposes of this book, just a fraction of these daily *adkhaar* have been captured in Tables 4.1 and 4.2:

Table 4.1 Adhkaar and virtue

Adhkaar *and virtue*	*Recommended number of times to recite*	*Recommended times to recite*
Last three chapters of the Qur'ân Abdullah ibn Khubayb reports that the Prophet (ﷺ) said: "… Recite *Qul huwallahu Ahad, Qul A'udhu bi Rabbil Falaq and Qul A'udhu bi Rabbin Nas,* thrice every morning and evening. It will suffice you for everything." (Abu Dawud; Tirmidhi). It was narrated from "Aishah that when the Prophet (ﷺ) went to bed every night, he would put his cupped hands together, then blow (dry spittle) into them, then recite into them the last three *surahs* of the Qur'ân, then he would wipe his hands over as much of his body as he could, starting with his head and face, and the front part of his body. He would do that three times." (Bukhari)	3 times	Morning and evening before sleeping
Ayat al kursi, **The Verse of the Throne** "Reading *Āyat al-Kursī* from *sūrah al-baqarah.* If you read it in the morning, you will be	1	

(*Continued*)

Table 4.1 (Continued)

Adhkaar *and virtue*	Recommended number of times to recite	Recommended times to recite
protected from us (i.e., the devils) till the evening. And if you read it in the evening, you will be protected from us (i.e., the devils) till the morning". (Ḥaakim)		
Whoever reads *ayat al kursi* after every obligatory prayer, there is nothing that will prevent him from entering Paradise except death (Nasaai).		
"When you lie down in your bed, recite *ayat al kursi* from beginning to end; a guardian angel will stay by you and no devil will approach you, until you wake up in the morning." (Bukhari)		
Ḥasbiyallāhu lā ilāha illā huwa `alayhi tawakkaltu, wa huwa Rabbu 'l-`Arshi 'l-`Aẓīm. "Allah is sufficient for me. There is none worthy of worship but Him. I have placed my trust in Him. He is the Lord of the Majestic throne." Allah will grant whoever recites this seven times in the morning or evening whatever he desires from this world or the next. (Abu Dawud in Hisnul Muslim)	7	Morning and evening
Bismillahil-ladhi la yadurru ma'as-mihi shai'un fil-a rdi wa la fis-sama'i, wa Huwas-Sami'ul-`Alim In the Name of Allah with Whose Name there is protection against every kind of harm in the earth or in the heaven, and he is the All-Hearing and All-Knowing	3	Morning and evening

(*Continued*)

Table 4.1 (Continued)

Adhkaar *and virtue*	*Recommended number of times to recite*	*Recommended times to recite*
The Prophet (🕌) said, "He who recites three times every morning and evening: '*Bismillahil-ladhi …* ,' nothing will harm him." (Abu Dawud; Tirmidhi)		
sayyidul stigfaar Whoever recites it in the morning, having utmost sincerity [hoping for forgiveness and reward], and then passes away on that day before entering the evening, will be among the people of *jannah* [i.e he/she will enter *jannah*]. And whoever recites it at night, having utmost sincerity, then passes away before entering the morning will be among the people of *jannah* (Bukhari).	1	Morning and evening
A'udhu bi kalimat Allaah al-taammaat min sharri ma khalaq "I seek refuge in the Perfect Words of Allah from the evil of what He has created." Narrated by at-Tirmidhi: "Whoever says three times when evening comes, '*A'oodhu bi kalimaat Allaah al-taammah min sharri ma khalaq* (I seek refuge in the perfect words of Allah from the evil of that which He has created)," no fever will harm him that night.	3	Morning and evening
Last two verses of *surah baqarah* The Prophet (🕌) said, "if somebody recited the last two verses of *surah al-baqarah* at night, that will be sufficient for him." (Bukhari)	1	Before sleeping

Source: Adapted from: Al-Qahtani, 2009.

Table 4.2 Prophetic supplication and virtue

Prophetic supplication and virtue	Transliteration	Translation
Supplication for protection from illness	*Allāhumma innī a'ūdhu bika min al-baraṣi wa-al-junūni wa-al-judhāmi wa-min sayyi'i al-asqām*	Oh Allah! I seek refuge in you from leucoderma, madness, leprosy, and evil diseases. [Abū Dāwūd and al-Nasa'ī]
Supplication in the time of hardship The Prophet (ﷺ) said, "so indeed, no Muslim supplicates with it for anything, ever, except Allah responds to him" (Tirmidhi).	*La ilaha illa anta subhanaka inni kuntu minaẓ-ẓalimin*	There is none worthy of worship except You, Glory to You, Indeed, I have been of the transgressors.
Supplication for protection from distress, hardship, and calamities	*Allaahumma 'innee 'a'oothu bika min jahdil-balaa'i, wa darakish-shaqaa'i,wa soo'il qadhaa'i, wa shamaatatil-'a'ada.*	"O Allah, I seek refuge in You from the anguish of tribulation, the lowest depths of misery, the bad of what is decreed and the malice of enemies" (Bukhari; Muslim)
Supplication when in distress This *dua* should also be read every morning and evening as part of daily *adkhaar*	*Ya Hayyu ya Qayyum, bi rahmatika astaghith, aslih li shani kullahu, wa la takilni ila nafsi tarfat 'ayn*	"Oh Allah, for Your mercy I hope, so do not leave me in charge of my affairs even for the blink of an eye; rectify all my affairs, there is no God but You."
Supplications for anxiety, sorrow, grief, depression, and anguish The Prophet (ﷺ) said, "There is no-one who is afflicted by distress and grief, and says the above dua but Allah will	*'Allaahumma Inni Abduka wa ibnu Abdik wa ibnu Amatik, Naasiyati biyadik, Maadhin Fiyya Hukmuk Adlun Fiyya Qadhaa'uk, As'aluka bi Killismin Huwa*	O Allah, I am Your slave, son of Your slave, son of Your maidservant; my forelock is in Your hand, Your command over me is forever executed and Your decree over me is just. I ask You by every

(Continued)

Table 4.2 (Continued)

Prophetic supplication and virtue	Transliteration	Translation
take away his distress and grief, and replace it with joy." (Ahmad)	*Lak, Sammayta bihi Nafsak Aw Allamtuhu Ahadan min Khalqik Aw Anzaltahu fi Kitaabik Aw ista'tharta bihi fi Ilmi al-Ghaybi Indak, an Tajal al-Qur'aana Rabeea Qalbi wa Noora Sadri wa Jalaa'a Huzni wa Thahaaba Hammi.*	name belonging to You which You have named Yourself with, or revealed in Your Book, or You taught to any of Your creation, or You have preserved in the knowledge of the Unseen with You, that You make the Qur'ân the life of my heart and the light of my breast, and a departure for my sorrow and a release for my anxiety
	Allaahumma 'innee 'a'oothu bika minal-hammi walhazani, wal'ajzi walkasali, walbukhli waljubni, wa dhala'id-dayni wa ghalabatir-rijaal	O Allah, I seek refuge in You from grief and sadness, from weakness and from laziness, from miserliness and from cowardice, from being overcome by debt and overpowered by men (i.e., others)." (Bukhari)
The Prophet (ﷺ) used to invoke Allah at the time of distress, saying	*"La ilaha illal-lahu Al-`Azim, al- Halim, La ilaha illal-lahu Rabbu-s-samawati wal-ard wa Rabbu-l-arsh il-azim."* (Bukhari)	There is none worthy of worship but Allah the Mighty, the Forbearing. There is none worthy of worship but Allah, Lord of the Magnificent Throne. There is none worthy of worship but Allah, Lord of the heavens and Lord of the earth, and Lord of the Noble Throne.

(Continued)

Table 4.2 (Continued)

Prophetic supplication and virtue	Transliteration	Translation
It was reported that Asmaa' bint 'Umays (may Allah be pleased with her) said: The Prophet (🕊) said to me: "Shall I not teach you some words to say when you feel distressed, depressed and worried." (Abu Dawud)	*Allah Allah Rabbi, laa ushriku bika shay'a*	Allah, Allah my Lord, I do not associate anything with Him.
Supplication when afraid to sleep, feeling lonely, or depressed. The Prophet (🕊) said: "whoever says upon leaving their house" the above *dua*, it will be said to him: 'You are guided, defended and protected.' The devil will go far away from him." (Tirmidhi)	*Bismillaahi, tawakkaltu 'alallaahi, wa laa hawla wa laa quwwata illaa billaah*	In the Name of Allah, I have placed my trust in Allah; there is no might and no power except by Allah.
Supplication for encompassing *aafiyah.* (well-being) is an encompassing word referring to overall well-being. This can include health, wealth, and safety from anything that may be deemed as harmful.	*Allahumma inni as'alukal-'afwa wal-'afiyah fid-dunya wal-akhirah*	Oh Allah, I ask You for forgiveness and well-being in this world and in the Hereafter.

Source: Adapted from: Al-Qahtani, 2009.

The Muslim practitioner and client

Based on the discussion above, the vast benefits offered by incorporating daily *adhkaar* into practice are undeniable. Muslim practitioners in the field of Islāmic psychology and Muslim mental health should optimise the use of *adhkaar* as a primary preventative-level intervention in therapeutic practice. Disregarding this divine gift would be a grave mistake due to its many psychological benefits. It is a well-known preventative measure for fear, anxiety, worry, sadness, reduction of stress, and an array of other forms of affliction as highlighted earlier. The tranquillity, calmness, and contentment that it brings to the heart will inspire hope, positivity, and healthy coping among clients (Nasrabadi et al., 2004; Azma et al., 2006).

The Islāmic psychotherapist and Muslim health practitioner, as a prerequisite, will be required to have the knowledge and understanding of *adhkaar* in order to educate, guide, and equip the client to incorporate this into their daily lives. Through the lens of the Western paradigm, this would parallel with the view of moving away from a predominantly pathogenic focus on clients to one that focuses on a strength based or "fortigenic" paradigm, which aims to optimise well-being before ill health or harm occurs (Strumpfer, 1995). Many studies have shown that the effect of remembering God and resorting to prayer influences the cognitive processes of the brain and consequently leads to lowering stress, heart rate, and blood pressure which ultimately allows individuals to face high-risk events appropriately (Hosini, 2008). In a further study by Rosmarin et al. (2009), it was found that the remembrance of God increases the feeling of well-being in psychological as well as mental dimensions, including anxiety, stress, and depression.

In concluding this chapter, a noteworthy point under the banner of *adkhaar* and remembrance of Alláh is the Islāmic psychology practitioner's incorporation of *du'ah and adkhaar* as part of their own daily routine for therapeutic practice. Seeking the guidance of Alláh before beginning a session with a client, adopting specific choices of *adkhaar* as a preparation for the session (or even discreetly during the session when faced with difficulty), and making this a consistent and conscious part of the practitioner's routine irrespective of the level of complexity in terms of the clients presenting problems. Some examples of specific choices of *adkhaar/ dua'h* include but are not limited to are presented in Table 4.3.

Table 4.3 Specific choices of *adkhaar/supplication*

Supplications	Transliteration
The dua 'h of Musa in Surah Taha when he was embarking on a very weighty task, "My Lord, expand for me my breast [with assurance] and ease for me my task and untie the knot from my tongue that they may understand my speech." (Taha 20:25–28)	Rabbish rahli sadri, wasyassirli amri,wahlul uqdathum millisaani, yafqahu qawli.

(*Continued*)

Table 4.3 (Continued)

Supplications	Transliteration
Oh, Alláh direct me to the right path and make me adhere to the Straight Path (Muslim cited in Al Qahtani, 2009).	*Allaahummah-dinee wa saddidnee.*
Oh Alláh, I ask You for guidance and uprightness/direction (Muslim cited in Al Qahtani, 2009).	Alláhum inni as'alukal huda, was sadaada.
O Alláh, I seek refuge in You lest I misguide others, or I am misguided by others, lest I cause others to err or I am caused to err, lest I abuse others or be abused, and lest I behave foolishly or meet with the foolishness of others" (Ibn Majah; Tirmidhi; An Nasai cited in Al Qahtani, 2009).	Allaahumma innee a'oodhu bika an adhilla, aw udhalla, aw azilla, aw uzalla, aw adhlima, aw udhlama, aw ajhala aw yujhala alayya.

It is hoped that the abovementioned discussion around *adhkaar* has contextualised its salient role as a primary preventative intervention, which can be incorporated and built into therapeutic practice by Islāmic psychotherapists and Muslim mental health practitioners easily and effectively.

References

Al-Jawziyyah, I. Q. (2020). *The disease and the cure: The sufficient answer for the one who asked about the remedial cure.* Philadelphia: Hikmah Publications.

Al-Qahtani, S. B. W. (2009). *Fortress of the Muslim. Invocations from the Quran and Sunnah (Hisnul Muslim Eng translation).* Riyadh: Darussalam Publications.

Azma, K., Jahangir, A., Etephagh, L., Enzavaee, A., Raeesosadat, A., Asheghan, M., & Motahary, A. (2006). Effect prayer of therapy on clinical symptoms and diagnostic findings in patients with carpal tunnel syndrome. *Journal of Army University of Medical Sciences, Iran*, 4, 791–794.

Basri, M. M. I. (2008). *Indahnya tawakal [The significance of tawakkul]*. Surakarta: Indiva Pustaka.

Huda, M., Sudrajat, A., Muhamat, R., Teh, K. S. M., & Jalal, B. (2019). Strengthening divine values for self-regulation in religiosity: Insights from Tawakkul (trust in God). *International Journal of Ethics and Systems*, 10.1108/IJOES-02-2018-0025

Hosini, M. (2008). Effect of prayer with emphasis on cognitive processes. Effects and benefits of pilgrimage, Seminar Proceedings pilgrimage. Retrieved from http://www.old.hajj.ir/hadjwebui/library/wfViewBookPage.aspx?bookId=1444

Islām Q&A (2018a). 145543: Dua before sleeping (List of sound hadith), Islām Question and Answer. Online at https://Islāmqa.info/en/answers/145543/dua-before-sleeping-list-of-sound-hadiths (accessed 7 August 2023).

Islām Q&A (2018b). 217496: Morning and evening adkhar, Islām question and answer. Online at https://Islāmqa.info/en/answers/217496/morning-and-evening-adhkar (accessed 7 August 2023).

Islām Q&A (2010a). 49030: What is the meaning of tawhid? Islām question and answer. Online at https://Islāmqa.info/en/answers/49030/what-is-the-meaning-of-tawhid (accessed 8 August 2023).

Islām Q&A (2010b). 22765: When to Read Evening Adhkar, Islām Question and Answer. Online at https://Islāmqa.info/en/answers/22765/when-to-read-evening-adhkar, (accessed 8 August 2023).

Morning Adhkar. (n.d.). Online at https://lifewithAlláh.com/dhikr-dua/main-adhkar/morning/ (accessed 7 August 2023).

Muslim. *Sahih Muslim* 2725a. In-book reference: Book 48, Hadith 104. USC-MSA web (English) reference: Book 35, Hadith 6573.

Nadeer, A. (2021). *The ruqya handbook: A practical guide to spiritual healing* (1st ed.). London: Al Ruqya Healing. Independently published.

Nasrabadi, N. A., Larijani, T. T., Mahmoudi, M., & Taghlili, F. A. (2004). Comparison of the effect of Benson relaxation methods and Azkar (Zikr) on the Anxiety levels of patients awaiting abdominal surgery. *Hayat*, 10, 29–37.

Qamar, A. H. (2013). The concept of the 'evil' and the 'evil eye' in Islām and Islāmic faith healing traditions. *Journal of Islāmic Thought and Civilisation*, 3(2), 44–53.

Rassool, G. Hussein. (2019). *Evil eye, jinn possession and mental health issues. An Islāmic perspective.* Oxford: Routledge.

Revive the Sunnah. (n.d.). Online at https://revivethe-sunnahs.com/Adkhartypes.html (accessed 8 August 2023).

Riyad. Riyad as-Salihin 1433. In-book reference: Book 15, Hadith 26. Online at https://sunnah.com/riyadussalihin:143 (accessed 7 August 2023).

Rosmarin, D., Pargament, K., & Mahoney, A. (2009). The role of religiousness in anxiety, depression, and happiness in a Jewish community sample: A preliminary investigation. *Mental Health, Religion and Culture*, 12, 97–113.

Strümpfer, D. J. W. (1995). The origins of health and strength: From "salutogenesis" to "fortigenesis." *South African Journal of Psychology*, 25(2), 81–89. 10.1177/008124639502500203

Ummah Welfare Trust. (2018). Daily adkhaar: Authentic remembrances and supplications as prescribed by the Messenger of Alláh (2nd ed.). Online at

https://uwt.org/wp-content/uploads/2018/10/Adkhar_
Book.pdf (accessed 8 August 2023).

Wyatt, T. (2020). Protective prayers for relief and
protection. Online at https://yaqeeninstitute.org/read/
paper/duas-for-relief-and-protection#ftnt4 (accessed
8 August 2023).

Yunus, M. (1990). *Kamus Bahasa Arab-Indonesia
[A dictionary of Arab to Indonesia]*. Jakarta: Bulan
Bintang.

5   *Ruqyah-ash-Shar'iah* as a spiritual intervention

Introduction

This chapter begins by emphasising the significance of *ruqyah-ash-Shar'iah* as a *sunnah*-based intervention for addressing various afflictions, encompassing spiritual, psychological, and physical issues. The distinction between permissible and impermissible *ruqyah* is explored, along with a presentation of the supporting evidence that validates the acceptability of *ruqyah*. Additionally, the conditions of *ruqyah* are described, and an explanation of the *ruqyah* process is provided, which can be shared with clients. The chapter's aim is to contextualise the role of Islāmic psychotherapists and Muslim mental health practitioners in applying *ruqyah* as a spiritual intervention. To illustrate this, a case study is presented, demonstrating how *ruqyah-ash-Shar'iah* was employed as a part of a comprehensive therapeutic practice.

What is *ruqyah*?

Ruqyah is a method of treating spiritual diseases by employing Qur'ānic recitations and invocations

DOI: 10.4324/9781003344827-5

as prescribed by the Messenger of Alláh (ﷺ) (Abdussalam Bali, 2004; Nadeer, 2021). It may also involve additional actions like blowing lightly or dry spitting after reciting Qur'ānic verses or Prophetic invocations. Etymologically, the term *ruqyah* derives from the root word *ouda*, which conveys the idea of turning towards or seeking refuge in something. This implies that *ruqyah* is a process used to seek healing, whether through permissible or impermissible means (Nadeer, 2021). *Ruqyah* is a comprehensive approach utilised to address a variety of issues, including curing the evil eye, countering the effects of magic, dealing with *jinn* possession, as well as treating physical and psychological ailments (Ameen, 2005; Nadeer, 2021). It encompasses a wide range of applications aimed at providing relief and healing for those suffering from different afflictions (Bhika & Dockrat, 2015; Nadeer, 2021). To provide a deeper understanding, let us refer to the statement by Ibn Al-Qayyim Al-Jawziyyah, who eloquently expressed the healing power of the Qur'ān. He mentions that "the Qur'ān is the most complete cure from all physical and psychological illnesses, as well as illnesses of this world and the illnesses of the Hereafter … If the sick person uses the proper method of using the Qur'ān as a medicine, with firm belief and faith, and he/she fulfils all of the conditions, no disease can overcome him/her. How can a disease overcome the speech of the Lord of the Heavens and the Earth, the speech which if it was sent upon a mountain, would shatter that mountain to dust from its greatness and its glory … There is no illness of the heart and the body except that the Qur'ān contains the means to protect and guide how to cure it … As for the diseases of the heart, Allāh mentions them in detail along with their causes and the method of curing them. So, the one who is not cured by the Qur'ān, may Allāh not cure him, and the one who the Qur'ān is not sufficient for him, may Allāh not suffice him in anything! It is well known from experience that words have particular effects and benefits on people, then what do you think of the speech of the Lord of the worlds, the One who the virtue of His speech over the speech of others, is like the virtue of Him over his creation. The Qur'ān is the perfect cure, and it is a beneficial means of protection, and a guiding light and a general mercy" (Al-Jawziyyah, 2010 cited in Islām Q&A, 2008).

In his book Zaad al-Ma'ad, Ibn Al-Qayyim Al-Jawziyyah elaborates on the remedies for sickness that the Prophet (ﷺ) used, classifying them into three types:

- Natural remedies: The Prophet (ﷺ) employed natural remedies to treat illnesses. These remedies were based on the natural resources available in the environment and the beneficial properties of various substances.
- Divine remedies: In addition to natural remedies, the Prophet (ﷺ) also used divine remedies, which included the recitation of specific Qur'ānic verses and Prophetic invocations. These remedies had a spiritual aspect, seeking Allāh's blessings and healing through the sacred words and supplications.
- Remedies composed of both: There were instances where the Prophet (ﷺ) combined natural

remedies with divine remedies. This approach encompassed using both the healing properties of certain substances found in nature and the spiritual power of Qur'ānic verses and invocations (Al-Jawziyyah, 2003).

Through these three types of remedies, the Prophet (ﷺ) provided holistic approaches to healing, addressing not only the physical aspects of sickness but also the spiritual and emotional dimensions, acknowledging the interconnection between body, mind, and soul in the healing process (Bhikha & Dockrat, 2015).

Categories of *ruqyah*

Ruqyah is a term used to encompass various types of incantations, but it can be divided into two distinct categories, each having significant differences and consequences. The first category is known as *ruqyah-ash-Shar'iah*, which falls under the realm of permissible *(halal)* practices. The second category is called *ruqyah-as-shirkiyyah*, which is considered impermissible (*haram*) due to its association with disbelief (*shirk*) (Nadeer, 2021; Yusuf, 2022). *Ruqyah-ash-Shar'iah* involves treating illnesses in all their forms using Qur'ānic and Prophetic invocations as prescribed by the Prophet (ﷺ). It is a legitimate method for countering the effects of the evil eye, magic, psychological and physical ailments, as well as diseases of the heart (Nadeer, 2021). It is crucial to establish this distinction from the outset because the first category adheres to the principles of Islāmic law

(*Shar'iah*), while the second category involves practices that contradict Islāmic beliefs and teachings. By understanding these differences, one can avoid the potential harms of engaging in impermissible *ruqyah-as-shirkiyyah* and instead seek the beneficial and permissible aspects of *ruqyah-ash-Shar'iah* in treating various afflictions (Nadeer, 2021). In addition to its healing properties, *ruqyah* serves as an effective means for Muslims to strengthen their faith and affirm their belief in the Oneness of Allāh (*tawheed*). Seeking treatment through the Qur'ān demonstrates a profound trust in the curative powers of Allāh's words. It also contributes to a person's spiritual journey and revives a significant Prophetic tradition (Abdussalam Bali, 2004). As evidenced by a *hadīth*, the Prophet (ﷺ) encouraged the use of two remedies: honey and the Qur'ān (Ibn Majah (a)). This emphasises the position of the Qur'ān as a healing source. Al-Qahtani (2009), a prominent scholar in this field, explains that *ruqyah-ash-Shar'iah* is not only permissible but also recommended. This is because it adheres to the guidelines laid out in the Qur'ānic verses and *hadīth*, while relying on the firm belief that Allāh is the ultimate healer who can alleviate any affliction.

By engaging in *ruqyah-ash-Shar'iah*, Muslims demonstrate their trust in Allāh's ability to heal and reaffirm their faith in the divine power of the Qur'ān, which is the words of Allāh. This practice aligns with the teachings of Islām and serves as a means to draw closer to Allāh during times of illness and distress (Al-Jawziyyah, 2010; Abdussalam Bali, 2004; 2015). Al Asqalani (1997) asserts that the permissibility of *ruqyah* is widely accepted among Muslim scholars, provided that certain conditions are met. These conditions are as follows:

Use of Alláh's words: The recitation in *ruqyah* should solely consist of verses from the Qur'ân, Alláh's Names, or His Attributes. This ensures that the practice is firmly rooted in the divine revelations and avoids any innovation or addition of non-Qur'ānic elements.

Language of recitation: The recitation should be in Arabic, the language of the Qur'ân, or if recited in another language, it must be comprehensible and understandable to the person seeking healing. This ensures that the individual can comprehend the meaning and significance of the recited verses.

• Belief in Alláh's facilitation: Those involved in the *ruqyah* process must firmly believe that the recitation itself does not possess an independent curative effect. Instead, they must understand that it is Alláh Almighty who facilitates the healing through His divine power and mercy (Nadeer, 2021; Yusuf, 2022).

It is crucial to note that the permissibility of *ruqyah* hinges on its adherence to the principles of Islām and its avoidance of any practices that may lead to disbelief (*shirk*). As long as the process of *ruqyah* aligns with the teachings of Islām and does not involve any acts of polytheism or contradiction to Islāmic beliefs, it remains permissible and beneficial for seeking healing and protection (Rahman & Hussein, 2021; Nadeer, 2021). Scholars hold two different opinions regarding the scope of *ruqyah,* whether it should be restricted to what is explicitly mentioned in the Qur'ān and *Sunnah* or if certain conditions should be met while allowing flexibility in its implementation (Rahman & Hussein, 2021). Those who do not restrict it emphasise the importance of adhering to specific conditions without compromise. This stance is supported by the *hadīth* of Awf Ibn Malik, which states that *ruqyah* is permissible as long as it does not involve associating partners with Alláh (*shirk*) (Muslim (a)). This suggests that any adopted methods of *ruqyah* that lack Prophetic tradition should avoid mysterious words, symbols within amulets, or chanting in incomprehensible languages. Additionally, the practice should not resemble the rituals of magicians, soothsayers, or pagan worshippers (Abdussalam Bali, 2004; 2015; Alruqyah healing, 2019).

Ruqyah is a practice closely linked to worship, and therefore, Muslims should exercise great caution in the methods they use. Whenever they encounter unfamiliar practices that are not in line with the traditions of the pious predecessors, especially the first three generations after the Prophet (﷽), they are advised to refer back to the Qur'ān and *Sunnah* for guidance (AbdussalamBali, 2004; Yusuf, 2022). This approach ensures that *ruqyah* remains pure and free from any form of innovation or deviation from Islāmic principles. By adhering to the teachings of the Qur'ān and the Prophetic traditions, Muslims can perform *ruqyah* with confidence, seeking Alláh's help and healing while avoiding any practices that may lead to deviation from the true path of Islām

(Nadeer, 2021; Al-Jawziyyah, 2010; Al Qahtani, 2009). Indeed, one should be cautious and avoid getting involved in mystical and mysterious methods that claim to be acceptable *ruqyah*. Impermissible *ruqyah* involves invoking beings other than Alláh, either explicitly or subtly. The most concerning aspect of this type of *ruqyah* is that it leads people to engage in practices, rituals, and incantations of disbelief (*shirk*) to seek the assistance of jinn (Nadeer, 2021).

Impermissible *ruqyah* adopts the same conditions and principles as magic *(sihr)*, which is considered one of the major sins in Islām. The Prophet Muhammad (ﷺ) emphasised that *an-nushrah*, which refers to using magic spells to counteract other magic spells, is a practice of *shaytan* (Abu Dawud (a)). Therefore, the concept of "white magic" or any form of permissible magic does not exist in Islām (Islām Q&A, 2014). When seeking impermissible *ruqyah* through others, individuals often approach magicians and soothsayers who have close associations with the *jinn* (Abdussalam Bali, 2004). The Prophet (ﷺ) warned against consulting fortune tellers and those who claim knowledge of the unseen, as their practices lead to disbelief in the revelations brought by Muhammad (ﷺ) (Ibn Majah (b)). Hence, anyone who believes in what these fortune tellers say has indeed rejected the teachings of Islām. The severity of seeking such assistance is highlighted by the narration that mentions how the prayer of the one who approaches a fortune teller for information from the unseen will not be accepted for 40 nights (Muslim (b)).

Muslims are urged to stay away from such practices and instead seek help and healing through permissible *ruqyah*, which is based on the Qur'ān and Prophetic traditions and emphasises complete trust in Alláh as the ultimate healer and source of all power (Abdussalam Bali, 2004).

Another predominant feature of impermissible *ruqyah* is that it usually is applied under strange conditions and requires a person to engage in bizarre ritualistic practices. This is usually to please the *jinn* who assists the magician in fulfilling the requirements (Abdussalam Bali, 2004; Rahman & Hussein, 2021). People who follow these practices under the guise of being religious, sometimes claim that these *jinn* are "Muslim *jinn*" or "good *jinn*" and justify these practices on this basis. A clear indication that suggests this is an incorrect and unacceptable approach to *ruqyah* is due to the narration in which the Prophet (﷽) related a profound occurrence in a *hadīth* relating to this matter. He said, "A strong demon from the jinn came to me yesterday suddenly, so as to spoil my prayer, but Alláh enabled me to overpower him, and so I caught him and intended to tie him to one of the pillars of the mosque so that all of you might see him, but I remembered the invocation of my brother Sulaiman: 'And grant me a kingdom such as shall not belong to any other after me.' (Saad, 38:35) so I let him go cursed" (Bukhari (a)). This *hadīth* not only confirms that the best of creation did not permit himself to restrain and order the *jinn* based on the kingdom that was only permitted to the Prophet Sulaiman (May Alláh be pleased with him), but it also clearly suggests that we as commonfolk cannot justify approving such involvement with the *jinn*.

Although there is a difference in opinion on the use of Qur'ānic amulets, there is no difference of opinion that when these amulets incorporate symbols or additional elements that contradict Islāmic beliefs, this becomes impermissible. Some amulets may include verses alongside invocations that seek help from angels, Prophets, or *jinn* instead of relying solely on Alláh for assistance. This mixing of beliefs can lead to practices of disbelief (*shirk*) and is against the principles of tawheed (Al-Jawziyyah, 2003; Islām Q&A, 2020). The Prophet Muhammad (ﷺ) explicitly warned against hanging up amulets, and he stated that whoever does so is guilty of disbelief (An-Nasai (a)). This authentic *hadīth* emphasises the seriousness of depending on amulets and the importance of avoiding any form of association of partners with Alláh in matters of worship and protection. Additionally, relying on objects like charms or so-called "objects of protection," such as seashells, dream catchers, bones, the eye of Fatima, lemons, and others, is impermissible in Islām. These practices involve seeking protection from sources other than Alláh, which contradicts the core belief that Alláh alone is the ultimate protector and provider of security (Yusuf, 2022; Al Jeraisy, 2001; Islām Q&A 2001).

Muslims are advised to steer clear of these practices and instead place their complete trust and reliance on Alláh in all matters of healing, protection, and seeking help. The use of pure and permissible *ruqyah*, adhering solely to the Qur'ān and *Sunnah*, is the recommended way to seek Alláh's blessings and assistance in times of difficulty and distress (Al-Jawziyyah, 2003; Al Jeraisy, 2001; Nadeer, 2021).

Evidences of *ruqyah* application from the Qur'ān and *Sunnah* for all forms of harm

The evidence for using Qur'ānic recitation for *ruqyah* and its effectiveness in treating physical, psychological, and spiritual diseases is established in the statements of Alláh:

يَـٰٓأَيُّهَا ٱلنَّاسُ قَدْ جَآءَتْكُم مَّوْعِظَةٌ مِّن رَّبِّكُمْ وَشِفَآءٌ لِّمَا فِي ٱلصُّدُورِ وَهُدًى وَرَحْمَةٌ لِّلْمُؤْمِنِينَ

- "mankind, there has to come to you instruction from your Lord and healing for what is in the breasts and guidance and mercy for the believers." (Yunus 10:57, interpretation of the meaning)

وَنُنَزِّلُ مِنَ ٱلْقُرْءَانِ مَا هُوَ شِفَآءٌ وَرَحْمَةٌ لِّلْمُؤْمِنِينَ وَلَا يَزِيدُ ٱلظَّـٰلِمِينَ إِلَّا خَسَارًا

- And We send down of the Qur'ān that which is healing and mercy for the believers, but it does not increase the wrongdoers except in loss. (Al-Israa 17:82, interpretation of the meaning)

قُلْ هُوَ لِلَّذِينَ ءَامَنُوا۟ هُدًى وَشِفَآءٌ

- Say, "It is, for those who believe, a guidance and cure." (Fussilat 41:44, interpretation of the meaning)

The verses above provide supporting evidence for the following points:

- The Qur'ān is a remedy for the ailments of the heart.
- From an Islāmic perspective, the heart (*qalb*) is considered the centre of misguidance, ignorance, false beliefs, desires, sadness, and depression.
- The level of righteousness or deviation in an individual is connected to the state of their heart.
- Allāh informs us that the Qur'ān serves as a cure for the heart, and thus, we should turn to it to seek healing for these afflictions.
- This also serves as clear proof that using the Qur'ān as a form of *ruqyah* is permissible and encouraged. Acting upon it and reciting it can be a means to seek healing for the issues affecting the heart. Moreover, the potential for cure and healing lies not only in specific verses but encompasses the entirety of the Qur'ān (Humble, n.d).

With regards to evidence from the *Sunnah*, there are many narrations which cover the aspect of the use of *ruqyah* for healing with regards to different forms of illness and harm. Below are some of these said narrations:

- It has been reported that Aisha mentioned, "The Prophet (☀) ordered me or someone else to do *ruqyah*, if there was danger from an evil eye" (Ibn Majah (c)). It was also narrated by Umm Salama that the Prophet (☙) saw in the house a girl whose face had a black spot. He said, "she is under the effect of the evil eye, so treat her with *ruqyah*"(Bukhari (b)). It was further narrated by Al Aswad; I asked Aisha about treating poisonous stings (snake bites or scorpion bites) with *ruqyah*. She said, "the Prophet (☙) allowed the treatment of poisonous stings with *ruqyah*" (Bukhari c)).

- Narrated from 'A'ishah that when any of the members of the Prophetic household fell ill Alláh's Messenger (☙) used to blow over them by reciting *mu'awwidhatain (surahs Falaq and Naas),* and when he suffered from illness of which he passed away, she used to blow over him and rubbed his body with his hand for his hand had greater healing power than her hand (Muslim (c)).
- Ibn Majah narrated from 'Ali, who said, The Prophet (☙) said, "The best medicine is the Qur'ān." (Islām Q&A, 2016).

From the above evidences, we can understand that the use of *ruqyah* as a remedy and treatment is not restricted to spiritual affliction only but rather can be applied to any presenting concern and can also be combined with other conventional treatments. Based on the evidence presented, it can be inferred that the use of *ruqyah*, which involves using the Qur'ān as a form of healing and remedy, is not limited solely to spiritual afflictions. Instead, it can be applied to any existing concerns or issues affecting an individual, including physical, emotional, or psychological problems. Additionally, *ruqyah* can be combined with other conventional treatments to complement and enhance the overall healing process.

The Islāmic psychotherapist and the *ruqyah* process

The successful implementation of any *ruqyah* process is contingent upon the conditions that are listed below. In this chapter we will explain the process to be shared with the client, enabling them to take responsibility for their own *ruqyah* journey. The client can choose to perform the process themselves or with the assistance of a family member/s. It is essential to emphasise that the role of the Islāmic psychotherapist and Muslim mental health practitioner is not that of a spiritual healer (*Raaqi*). Instead, the practitioner acts as a facilitator, imparting the necessary information and details with regards to the process and providing support and motivation to the client as they embark on this journey.

To help with the assessment for *ruqyah*, a practical tool called the *Ruqyah* Indicator is introduced (refer to Table 5.1). This tool takes the form of a general questionnaire or guide, which the Islāmic psychotherapist can utilise before proceeding with the *ruqyah* process. It serves as a preliminary screening tool for the possibility of spiritual afflictions but should not be considered a definitive tool for spiritual diagnosis. Its purpose is merely to provide an indication of potential spiritual issues and may point the Muslim mental health practitioner towards incorporating a *ruqyah* programme as part of the therapeutic intervention.

Table 5.1 Ruqyah indicator checklist

1 How long have you been experiencing these symptoms?
2 Do you experience any other symptoms? If so, describe them?
3 Do you experience headaches, or heavy headedness?
4 Do you experience tingling sensations in your hands or feet, or both?
5 Do you dream of animals or reptiles, falling from heights, drowning, teeth falling, brakes failing in car, or anything of similar nature?
6 Do you have any reaction to when the *adhaan* goes on, a dislike, or fear or sense of not wanting to listen?
7 Do you feel despondent in *salaah* or when reciting or listening to the Quran?
8 Do you ever see shadows at the corner of your eye and when you look there is nothing there?
9 Do you have any pain in the stomach area?
10 Do you have ringing in your ears?
11 Do you want to spend lots of unnecessary periods of time in the bathroom?
12 Do you feel the need to isolate yourself from everything and everyone?
13 Do you feel a sense of despair?
14 Do you have strength that isn't necessarily usual?
15 Are your moods erratic? For example: happy to irritable to angry to depressed, all without founded reason?
16 Do you find difficulty sleeping a full night, with broken unrested sleep?
17 Do you ever dream or feel semi-conscious while asleep and experience a sense of chest constriction, difficulty breathing, or screaming out
18 Do you have sexual dreams which may almost seem real?

(Continued)

Table 5.1 (Continued)

19 Do you have issues with low blood pressure, iron deficiency, and fainting?
20 Do you have shaking, pain, tightness, heaviness in different parts of your body, sometimes areas change without any specific pattern?
21 Do you feel like there is a pattern of things going wrong in your life?
22 Do you feel a sense of feeling stuck, or shackled in any way or form?
23 Do you have uncontrollable thoughts about Allah, the Prophet (ﷺ) Islam or d*een* related matters that you feel is out of character and makes you feel terrible to think about? (if clients says yes, please take steps to make them feel at ease in knowing this isn't their fault and Allah does not punish what is not acted upon, it is also a sign of a true believer, one who may have these thoughts but hates them and does not follow up with them).
24 Do you have a fear of anything in particular?
25 Do you hear voices?
26 Do you cry or laugh without reason?
27 Do you have thoughts of suicide or suicidal ideation?
28 Do you have a moving pain between the head neck and shoulders?
29 Do you have severe forms of fatigue, tiredness, and exhaustion?
30 Do you have dizziness or haziness in vision?
31 Is there anything else that you feel you could tell me that may or may not seem to make sense or feels strange for you that you may be experiencing?

The programme empowers the client to take responsibility for their own *ruqyah* process encouraging active engagement and ownership, fostering a more effective and holistic healing journey.

When and if the situation requires a more concerted, professional *ruqyah* intervention, the practitioner should have the required referral details of a reputable local *raaqi* or sheikh who could assist in the process. The practitioner's role, therefore, lies in being supportive, providing the necessary tools and knowledge, and not playing the role of both psychotherapist and *raaqi* (unless otherwise trained) while respecting the client's autonomy and choice throughout the *ruqyah* process.

If the client's answers to the questions in the *ruqyah* indicator predominantly indicate a potential spiritual affliction and there are no apparent medical, scientific, pharmacological, or psychological reasons for the client's current state, then directing the client towards *ruqyah* will certainly be beneficial. However, even if only a few of the questions are answered affirmatively, suggesting that *ruqyah* should still be considered as a potential intervention. This implies that the decision to recommend *ruqyah* should not solely rely on a strict yes-or-no interpretation of this questionnaire or any other tool, nor should the role of *ruqyah* as an intervention be restricted to spiritual affliction alone, as discussed throughout this chapter.

Below are points to take into consideration and explain to the client before they formally begin the *ruqyah* process:

• Intention: The intention should always be to ask Alláh to remove the harm or said affliction through the recitation and application of the *ruqyah*.

- Conviction: One should recite loudly and clearly, with firm conviction, belief, and trust in Alláh, who alone gives cure.
- Patience and consistency: Like any treatment, consistency is key. Daily recitation, *dua,* and other treatments must be maintained consistently for favourable results, even if it is just for a short period on a daily basis (Life with Alláh, 2013; Yusuf, 2022).

Before the *ruqyah*

- Assert Alláh's *tawheed* and understand that no healing is possible except with His permission and facilitation.
- Ablution is advised, along with two units of prayer and sincere *dua* at any time in the day or night.
- An absolute prerequisite would be to correct one's position with regards to the compulsory acts of worship and ensure that this is in place. An analogy that can be used to explain the wisdom behind this is that of a house without a roof. We can try to shut the windows and doors (*ruqyah*), but if there is no roof (compulsory acts of worship, e.g., *salah*, we will not prevent the house from all the dangers and harms that could potentially enter.
- Placing the focus on asking for forgiveness from Alláh and try one's best to stay away from the major sins.
- Give attention to the rights of people who you have duties towards and try to remedy situations

if you have wronged them or acted unjustly in any way.

- Give charity as it wards off calamity. The Messenger of Alláh (ﷺ) said, "Treat your sick by giving charity" (Bayhaqi cited in Islām Q&A, 2016).
- Remove animate pictures, amulets containing illegible text or invoking upon other than Alláh should also be taken out and disposed of in the correct manner (Life with Alláh, 2023).

During the *ruqyah*

- Recite the *ruqyah* loudly, clearly, and with concentration at 1,3,5, or any odd number of times.
- Recite directly into your hands, dry-spitting (*nafth*) into them and rubbing them over the body. You or a family member (*mahram* if of opposite gender) may also recite while placing your hands over the part of the body that is in pain (Nadeer, 2021).
- Recite and blow on water, olive oil, or black seed oil in a similar manner by keeping your mouth close to the vessel and intermittently dry spitting into it. The more convicted the person reciting the *ruqyah* is, the stronger the effect of the *ruqyah*. To understand this, we can allude to a metaphor. The sword is sharp enough to strike the enemy, but the person holding the sword needs to have the strength to apply its function. The *ruqyah* water can be used for drinking and bathing, and the oils can be used to anoint the body as and where required (Ummah Welfare Trust, 2019; Nadeer, 2021).

- There is an effect behind blowing/dry-spitting when performing *ruqyah*. This form of blowing can be done by both pure and evil souls, as Alláh refers in the chapter on daybreak:

$$\text{وَمِن شَرِّ ٱلنَّفَّٰثَٰتِ فِي ٱلْعُقَدِ}$$

- *And from the evil of the blowers in knots."* (Al Falaq, 113:4, interpretation of the meaning)

- Those who work with magic tie knots and blow onto them by reciting words of magic and disbelief, and this affects the victim even in their absence. However, the righteous souls counter this by blowing with the powerful words of the Almighty (adapted from Al-Jawziyyah, 2003).
- When reciting on others or if others recite over you, place your hand (or have them place their hand) on the forehead of the affected person (maḥram, spouse, person of same gender, or child), or on the part of the body in pain, then recite and blow (dry spitting motion) on the person.
- If one cannot recite for whatever reason, then *ruqyah* can be listened to using headphones, preferably with full concentration (Life with Alláh, 2023).

After the *ruqyah*

- The client should keep a journal noting down how they feel during and after the *ruqyah* particularly with regards to the presenting problem.

For example, if the client is struggling with anxiety, they should take note of how they felt during the *ruqyah* as well as how they feel after it. It is possible, especially in the case of psychological manifestations of evil eye and magic, that symptoms become more profound during, and for a while after the *ruqyah*. Keeping a journal of these symptoms and effects of the *ruqyah* can help both the client and the practitioner (and if the practitioner does not feel confident enough, a consulting *raaqi,* with the consent of the client) identify potential patterns of affliction. This could then warrant a more concerted approach to focussing on the *ruqyah* process and potentially taking it a level further by incorporating prophetic remedies, increasing the time spent on it, and including further verses or chapters from the Qur'ān.

Addressing concerns related to spiritual affliction can indeed be challenging for the Islāmic psychotherapist or mental healthcare professionals due to the diverse cultural, religious, and medical perspectives on this matter. Sensitivity to the cultural and religious beliefs of clients is essential for promoting their mental and physical well-being. When there is a conflict between medicine and culture/religion, it can negatively impact the therapeutic alliance (Khalifa & Hardie, 2005). In cases of suspected spiritual affliction, it is crucial for the mental healthcare or Islāmic psychotherapist to conduct a thorough assessment of the client's physical symptoms. This should involve medical examinations and tests to rule out any valid scientific or medical underlying causes before considering spiritual interventions.

Below is a case study demonstrating the application of the remembrance of Alláh, *ruqyah-ash-Shar'iah,* and Prophetic Medicine as part of a therapeutic intervention in an Islāmic psychology setting. The case study includes a brief profile of the client, an explanation of the symptoms, and presenting issues, which initially appeared as medical problems. The proposed intervention by the Islāmic psychology practitioner is discussed, as well as the conclusion and outcome of the intervention, with the success attributed to Alláh's permission and the consistent practice of *ruqyah.* This case study highlights the importance of integrating cultural and religious aspects into the therapeutic process and how spiritual interventions can be effective in addressing certain conditions, as perceived by the client. However, it also emphasises the necessity of ensuring that medical evaluations are conducted to eliminate any underlying medical concerns before proceeding with spiritual interventions.

Case study

The client was a 38-year-old female medical doctor belonging to the Malay community in South Africa. She had no underlying medical conditions and had previously sought psychological therapy from the same Islāmic psychotherapist for various issues, including anxiety, trauma, family, and social concerns. These issues were effectively resolved through therapy. In 2021, the client suddenly fell seriously ill, experiencing physical symptoms such as vomiting, weakness, and paralysis in the lower part of her body, along with bladder and bowel dysfunction. She had received the COVID-19 vaccine two and a half months before falling ill and had also taken the flu vaccine about two weeks prior to her illness. Medical doctors diagnosed her with a rare condition called transverse myelitis, which involves inflammation of the spinal cord. However, despite numerous medical tests, the exact cause of her condition remained unidentified. The doctors informed her that it was unlikely she would regain the ability to walk independently.

Upon learning about her illness, the family engaged in various spiritual practices, including prayers, giving charity (*sadaqa*), sacrificing live animals, feeding the poor, and arranging for a minor pilgrimage (*umrah*) to be performed on her behalf. The client received some treatment at the hospital and was later transferred to a rehabilitation facility to work on regaining maximum functionality and learning to walk again. Unfortunately, on the first night at the rehabilitation facility, she experienced a severe and excruciating abdominal pain, further complicating her condition. In that week, her spouse, also a medical doctor, came in for an Islāmic therapy session and was advised by the Islāmic psychotherapists to consider alternative therapies for his wife such as *ruqyah-ash-Shar'iah* and the process was thoroughly explained. The spouse rationalised that it was another form of prayer which could help his wife although, at the time did not think that the cause of the illness could be related to spiritual affliction.

Due to the logistics of being in hospital and concerns with COVID 19, the spouse was not able to perform the *ruqyah* in person on a daily basis but was encouraged by the Islāmic psychotherapists to recite the *ruqyah* at home with the intention of healing and blow into water for her to drink and to bath with. The *ruqyah* document which contained verses from the Qur'ān and *Sunnah* was sent to the spouse to begin the process. The intention was made for cure from all physical illness as well as possible spiritual affliction such as black magic, evil eye, envy, and *jinn* possession.

The following verses from the Qur'ān were recited as part of the intervention:

• Surah Al-Fatiha
• Ayattul Kursi
• Al-Baqarah 2: 255
• The three Quls (Surah Al-Ikhlas, Al-Falaq, and An-Nas)
• The first five and last three verses of Al-Baqarah
• Verse 102 of Surah Al-Baqarah
• Other Qur'ānic verses related to black magic and healing

The method involved reading these verses and blowing into water, which the affected person would then drink and use for bathing. Additionally, the client's spouse was instructed to recite the same Qur'ānic verses on olive oil and/or black seed oil, which would then be applied to the areas where the client experienced pain or discomfort. This intervention was performed as part of the therapeutic approach to address the client's condition and seek healing through spiritual means. During the initial evening of the *ruqyah* process, the client's spouse experienced significant effects. He developed headaches, extreme exhaustion, and signs of irritability. He also faced challenges in getting out of bed and staying awake. Despite these difficulties, the spouse persisted in reading *ruqyah* on water for about two weeks and encouraged his wife to drink and bathe with it while she was at the rehabilitation facility. However, the *ruqyah* process was eventually interrupted and not sustained. As part of the treatment, the consumption of a certain variety of dates from the Holy City of Madinah, referred to as *ajwa* dates, was included in the treatment due to their known benefits in healing, especially in relation to afflictions.

While the client was at the rehabilitation facility, the institution became overwhelmed with the latest wave of COVID-19, prompting her spouse to bring her home and continue her rehabilitation as an outpatient. However, the happiness of having her home was short-lived, as the client started to deteriorate the following morning, and her condition showed no visible improvement over the next few weeks. Due to the severity of the COVID-19 wave, the client was reluctant to return to the rehabilitation facility. Over the next six weeks, her condition progressively worsened, leading her spouse, who is a doctor, to take matters into his own hands. He conducted blood tests, and with consultation from specialists at home, he also arranged for X-rays and scans to be performed on his wife. The test results indicated that hospitalisation was necessary. Consequently, she was admitted the next day in a severe septic condition. It was discovered that she had a severe infection of her heart valves, which had spread to her leg, spleen, bone marrow, and other areas. Urgent vascular surgery was required to remove the infection from her leg arteries in an attempt to save her limb. During this time, *Zam-Zam* water from a well in the city of Makkah, known for its healing properties had been recited into, and was used to wipe over the area of her heart as part of the treatment.

The situation had become critical, and medical interventions were necessary to address the severe infection and its spread to different parts of her body. The use of *Zam-Zam* water was incorporated as a spiritual element during this challenging time. During this period, the client underwent several surgeries, including open-heart surgery, as her condition was severely complicated with heart failure, sepsis, anaemia, malnutrition, and other complications. The surgery itself was successful in addressing some of the immediate concerns. However, throughout her seven-week hospital stay, she faced an array of highly rare, unusual, unexpected, and unexplained life-threatening complications. The medical team, including experienced professors and specialists in the field, were utterly perplexed and baffled by the unusual and unprecedented nature of her complications.

Despite their expertise and extensive knowledge, they could not provide any satisfactory explanations for the series of complications the wife experienced during her hospitalisation.

The situation was challenging and perplexing, as medical professionals grappled with the mystery of the wife's condition and sought to find answers to the unusual circumstances surrounding her health. Despite their best efforts, the cause of these rare complications remained elusive, leaving everyone involved in a state of uncertainty and concern. The complications from the leg surgery included damage to her nerves, affecting both her spinal cord and femoral nerve. As a result, she became immobile and bedbound, further worsening her prognosis for walking. After spending seven weeks in the hospital, she was discharged, but she still required a wheelchair and a walker for mobility. She would later relapse, forming a pattern of fluctuating health.

At this critical juncture, her spouse decided to restart the *ruqyah* process with greater focus and commitment. Having her at home made it easier to implement the process consistently, as he now had direct access to her. The spouse believed that the *ruqyah* process might provide some spiritual healing and relief, and he was determined to make a more sustained effort to help his wife's condition. The consistent implementation of *ruqyah* was seen as a potential avenue to address the complex and challenging health issues she was facing. The *ruqyah* process followed by the spouse involved specific prayers performed between late afternoon (*Asr*) and early evening (*Maghrib*), with the intention of seeking his wife's complete healing and the removal of any negative influences such as magic, evil eye, *jinn* interference, all forms of evil, known or unknown illnesses, and any calamities that may be affecting her (a comprehensive and all-encompassing intention). During the recitation, the spouse maintained deep concentration, earnestness, and sincerity, ensuring there were no disruptions. The *ruqyah* became an integral part of both the client's and his wife's daily routine, integrated into her treatment.

Interestingly, the wife exhibited noticeable reactions to the *ruqyah* process. For instance, she would enter into a deep, unconscious type of sleep during the recitation. Additionally, certain verses had more remarkable effects on her. Surah Baqarah verse 102 consistently elicited a response, causing her left leg to move (jerking) uncontrollably, akin to a focal seizure. She would be unaware of these physical reactions and have no recollection of them afterward. Furthermore, other verses, such as Ayatul Kursi, Surahs an-Naas and al-Falaq, and the last ten verses of Surah al-Baqarah, would also initiate reactions in her. The spouse continued to repeat and read these verses until the physical reactions ceased.

The spouse's consistent efforts in performing the *ruqyah*, along with his wife's reactions to specific verses, indicated the potential significance and impact of spiritual interventions in her healing journey. The process of *ruqyah* became a vital and dynamic aspect of her treatment, providing hope for a possible resolution to her complex health challenges. The *ruqyah* process was conducted for a substantial duration, typically lasting between 45 minutes to an hour. During this time, the spouse would recite the *ruqyah* and blow into his hands as well as over his wife. He would wipe his hands over the affected areas, which were primarily her left leg and heart region. Additionally, the spouse would read and blow into a mixture of olive oil and black seed oil, applying it to the affected leg, chest, and sometimes the abdomen in the morning. Furthermore, *ruqyah* was recited on *Zam-Zam* water or any other water that she consumed or used for bathing.

This consistent *ruqyah* process continued for months, leading to visible and measurable improvements in her health. Notable improvements included the restoration of normal bladder function, healing of leg injuries, and increased strength in her muscles. As her condition improved, the client regained the ability to read numerous supplications and verses of the Qur'ān by herself, reflecting the progress she had made in her healing journey. The dedicated and persistent application of *ruqyah*, combined with spiritual remedies like the recitation on oil and water, played a significant role in terms of her recovery and the positive changes observed in her overall health. These improvements not only manifested physically but also had a notable impact on her ability to engage in religious practices, further reflecting the holistic nature of her healing process. During the recovery period, while the couple continued with the *ruqyah* process, they experienced many disturbing dreams. These dreams involved being attacked by various creatures such as snakes, rats, crocodiles, lions, and hyenas. Additionally, the client had a dream where a group of *jinn* attacked her, but she managed to chase them away in her dream, often reciting the verses of *Ayatul Kursi* from the Qur'ān for protection. Throughout these evenings, the *ruqyah* water was used as a means of treatment and healing.

Despite these challenging dreams, her physical condition continued to improve. She grew stronger and healthier, progressing from praying in bed to praying while seated in a chair, and eventually, she was able to pray while standing. Her overall nutritional status and general health improved significantly, allowing her to safely observe fasting during appropriate times. Interestingly, as the client's condition improved and word spread about her progress, the leg spasms she previously experienced reemerged. These spasms were excruciating and at times disabling. However, her conviction to reciting her daily *adhkaar* and continuing with the *ruqyah* and olive oil/black seed oil applications remained steadfast. The recurrence of leg spasms highlights the complexity of the healing process and the need for continued dedication to spiritual practices and remedies. Despite the challenges, her determination to engage in spiritual practices like *ruqyah* and *adhkaar* played a significant role in her ongoing progress, improvement, and mainte-nance of her health. The combination of spiritual and physical healing methods contributed to her remarkable journey from weakness to strength. During the recovery period, the client experienced some peculiar episodes that were beyond medical explanation:

- At her workplace, she reported feeling a sensation of something being blown into her eyes, leading to temporary loss of vision. The only thing that seemed to alleviate this issue was reciting *Ayatul Kursi.*
- On two occasions, she experienced total leg weakness and paralysis. Again, the recitation of *Ayatul Kursi* appeared to be the remedy for this unusual symptom.

With no medical explanation for these episodes, the family continued their focus on the *ruqyah* water, using it for drinking and bathing purposes. Sometimes, they added (lote) *sidr* powder to the water as well. Additionally, they regularly played Surah Baqarah in their home and cleaned their living space with *ruqyah* water. The family remained committed to incorporating *Sunnah* healing methods into their treatment plan, following the advice of the Islāmic psychology practitioner. This included using honey, black seed oil, olive oil, *Zam-Zam* water, and dates. Furthermore, they integrated the practice of cupping therapy (*hijama*) into their treatment plan. Initially, wet cupping was avoided due to the client's use of blood thinners and the presence of a prosthetic heart valve, as there was a risk of bleeding complications. Instead, they adopted the practice of dry cupping, combining it with the recitation of the *ruqyah* verses on the *sunnah* days of the month.

The family's approach to treatment combined spiritual remedies, *Sunnah* practices, and conventional methods, reflecting their holistic approach to healing and their determination to find solutions for the client's health issues. This comprehensive treatment plan aimed to address both the physical and spiritual aspects of her condition, leading to continued progress in her recovery. Indeed, this case study provides a fascinating example of how *ruqyah-ash-Shar'iah*, the practice of Qur'ānic healing, was used by medical professionals to address potential spiritual affliction when conventional medical science could not provide answers or a complete healing for the condition they were experiencing. It highlights the importance of considering the spiritual and holistic aspects of healing, especially when faced with complex and unexplained health issues.

Spiritual affliction and Muslim mental healthcare

Mental health services and treatment interventions need to be inclusive in terms of the cultural and religious influences and the worldview of Muslim patients and clients in this regard. The diagnosis of patients struggling with the evil eye, black magic, or *jinn* possession which sometimes manifest as psychotic or psychological disorders may lead to the medicalisation of spiritual problems (Rassool, 2019). This increasing trend of medicalisation of these spiritual afflictions strictly reflects the Western paradigm of conceptualisation and understanding of spiritual diseases as limited to a medical model

(Rassool, 2019). Although it is necessary and important to resort to medical intervention, even in the event of spiritual affliction which manifest medically or psychologically, it is also very important to incorporate spiritual healing modalities such as *adhkaar* and *ruqyah* as part of more comprehensive and holistic healing approach. It has been suggested "that the medicalisation and psychiatrisation of various existential problems, which can be seen in subsequent editions of the DSM, encourages pathologising approach towards religious or spiritual problems" (Prusak, 2016, p. 175).

It is important to therefore note, that there are deeply entrenched historical differences and common mistrusts between religion and the field of psychiatry which has hampered collaboration between the two sectors (Patel, 2011). Religious beliefs regarding certain elements such as the evil eye, *jinn* possession, and black magic are matters of great contention among these mental healthcare practitioners which is further exacerbated by their Eurocentric biases and bridging the gap between the secular understanding and worldview of mental health problems and the spiritual worldview is a complex undertaking. A key barrier towards a process of collaboration centres around Imams and faith healers and the diversity regarding methods of intervention that are used, as well as their lack of knowledge regarding psychosocial interventions, including basic counselling, which prevents them from adequately fulfilling their role (Morgan, 2010). This is an important aspect and the deficit in this regard needs to be addressed. One of the most significant issues around mental health in Muslim communities stems from mistrust and stigma, and in this context Imams and faith leaders need to raise the issue of stigma and increase Muslim awareness of mental health and seeking assistance (Patel, 2011).

Regarding future research, Rahman (2014) suggests the importance of developing evidence-based *ruqyah* to assess the effectiveness of this therapeutic process. He emphasises that such research should not revolve around measuring *jinn* or religious beliefs, but rather should focus on evaluating the therapeutic impact of *ruqyah* therapy on individuals' health. "This approach aligns with the methods used to evaluate other evidence-based therapies or treatments" (Rahman, pp. 12–13). Furthermore, Rahman (2014) highlights a growing number of cases where patients have been treated with psychotropic medications without experiencing notable or definitive health improvements. In contrast, these same patients showed significant enhancement in their condition following *ruqyah* therapy. The case study presented earlier serves as a tangible illustration of this phenomenon, demonstrating a successful therapeutic outcome attributed to *ruqyah* therapy. Psychosocial intervention strategies should not be considered in isolation but rather from a comprehensive perspective that encompasses a range of approaches, including pharmacological/medical, psychosocial, and spiritual interventions (Prusak, 2016). As we have previously emphasised, it is essential to offer culturally appropriate services that cater to the specific needs of Muslim communities. Moreover, health practitioners must recognise that the delivery of culturally competent and congruent care is not only a professional obligation but also an ethical imperative (Rassool, 2019). By embracing a holistic and culturally sensitive approach, mental health professionals can better address the diverse needs and backgrounds of their clients, fostering a more inclusive and effective healing process.

Muslim mental healthcare practitioners encounter diverse challenges, and it is essential for them to focus on effective approaches and strategies that cater to the unique needs of their Muslim clientele. This includes placing greater emphasis on religious and cultural salience in their practice (Rassool, 2019). Understanding spiritual diseases and various forms of spiritual affliction is imperative for clinicians to gain insight into this often disregarded and stigmatised area. Unfortunately, some clinicians may hold biased and negative perceptions of their Muslim clients, and in some cases, they may altogether avoid discussing spiritual affliction due to a lack of knowledge and experience in this domain of client engagement (Patel, 2011).

To better serve their Muslim clients, mental healthcare practitioners must address these challenges and work towards fostering a more inclusive and culturally competent approach to treatment. Emphasising the importance of religious and cultural factors, and gaining understanding in the area of spiritual affliction, can facilitate more effective and holistic care for Muslim individuals seeking mental health support. By overcoming misconceptions and biases, clinicians can create a supportive and understanding therapeutic environment that meets the unique needs of their Muslim clientele.

References

Abdussalam Bali, W. (2004). *Sword against black magic & evil magicians*. (C. Abdelghani, Trans.). London UK: Al-Firdous Ltd.

Abdussalam Bali, W. (2015). *The cutting edge: How to face evil sorcerers*. (H. Kreidly, Trans). London UK: Dar Al Kotob Al-Ilmiyah.

Abu Dawud. *Sunan Abu Dawud*. 3868. In-book reference: Book 29, Hadith 14. USC-MSA web (English) reference: Book 28, Hadith 3859.

Al-Asqalani, A. B. A. I. H. (1997). *Fath al bari sharh sahih al bukhari: muqadimah*. Saudi Arabia: Dar al Salaam Publishers.

Al-Jawziyyah, I. Q. (2003). *Mukhtasar Zad Al Maad [Provisions of the hereafter]*. 1st edition. Saudi Arabia: Dar al Salaam Publishers.

Al-Jawziyyah, I. Q. (2010). From the Treasures of Ibnul Qayyim (1): A chapter on the Dispraise of Al-Hawa (lowly desire). Dar al-Khair.

Al- Jeraisy, K. (2001). (n.d). *Self ruqya treatment: Do it yourself and treat your family. Mohamed. M.A.M. (Trans)*. Riyadh, Saudi Arabia: The Believers Provision Series Book 5.

Al-Qahtani, S. B. A. (2009). *Supplications and treatment with ruqyah from the Quran and the Sunnah*. Riyadh, Saudi Arabia: Darussalam.

Al Ruqya Healing. (2019). *Ruqya. Al Ruqya healing*. https://www.ruqyainlondon.com (accessed 17 May 2023).

An-Nasai. *Sunan An-Nasai* 5067. In-book reference: Book 48, Hadith 28. Vol. 6, Book 48, Hadith 5070.

Ameen, A. M. K. I. I. (2005). *The Jinn and Human Sickness: Remedies in Light of the Quran and Sunnah.* Saudi: Darussalam Publications.

Bhika, R. & Dockrat, A. (2015). *Medicine of the prophet: Tibb Al- Nabawi, your guide to healthy living. South Africa*: Ibn Sina Institute of Tibb.

Bukhari. *Sahih al-Bukhari* 3423. In-book reference: Book 60, Hadith 95. USC-MSA web (English) reference: Vol. 4, Book 55, Hadith 634.

Bukhari. Sahih al-Bukhari 5739. In-book reference: Book 76, Hadith 54. USC-MSA web (English) reference: Vol. 7, Book 71, Hadith 63.

Bukhari. *Sahih al-Bukhari* 5741. In-book reference: Book 76, Hadith 56.USC-MSA web (English) reference: Vol. 7, Book 71, Hadith 637.

Humble, M. T. (n.d). Notes from Muhammad Tim's lectures: *Ruqyah*, the jinn, magic, evil eye and related topics. https://notes.muhammadtim.com/, (accessed 17 May 2023).

Ibn Majah. *Sunan Ibn Majah* 3452. In-book reference: Book 31, Hadith 17. Vol. 4, Book 31, Hadith 3452.

Ibn Majah. *Sunan Ibn Majah* 639. In-book reference: Book 1, Hadith 373. Vol. 1, Book 1, Hadith 63.

Ibn Majah. *Sunan Ibn Majah* 3512. In-book reference: Book 31, Hadith 77. Vol. 4, Book 31, Hadith 3512.

Islām Q&A. (2001). 'Ruling on wearing amulets for protection' Islām question and answer. https://IslāmQ&A.info/en/10543 (accessed 22 July 2023).

Islām Q&A. (2008). '9691: The Quran and medicine' Islām question and answer. https://IslāmQ&A.info/en/9691 (accessed 07/04/2023).

Islām Q&A. (2014). '181342: There is no good magic in Islām' Islām question and answer. https://IslāmQ&A.info/en/181342 (accessed 26 July 2023).

Islām Q&A. (2016). 'Offering the udhiyah with the intention of seeking healing' Islām question and answer. https://IslāmQ&A.info/en/107549 (accessed 22 July 2023).

Islām Q&A. (2020). 'About the words of the prophet saw recite your ruqyah s to me there is nothing wrong with a ruqyah that does not involve Shirk' Islām question and answer. https://IslāmQ&A.info/en/ 209745, (accessed 25 July 2023).

Khalifa, N., & Hardie, T. (2005). Possession and Jinn. *Journal of the Royal Society of Medicine*, 98(8), 351–353.

Life with Alláh (2023). Dhikr and dua. Life with Alláh. https://lifewithAlláh.com/articles/ruqyah/what-is-ruqyah (accessed 9 April 2023).

Morgan, J. (2010). *Muslim clergy in America: Ministry as profession in the Islāmic community (2nd edition)*. Lima, OH: Wyndham Hall Press.

Muslim. Sahih Muslim 2192a. In-book reference: Book 39, Hadith 68. USC-MSA web (English) reference: Book 26, Hadith 5439.

Muslim. Sahih Muslim 2192b. In-book reference: Book 39, Hadith 69. USC-MSA web (English) reference: Book 26, Hadith 5440.

Muslim. Sahih Muslim 2200. In-book reference: Book 39, Hadith 36.USC-MSA web (English) reference: Book 26, Hadith 5457.

Nadeer, A. (2021). *The Ruqya Handbook: A Practical Guide For Spiritual Healing*. Amazon Digital Services LLC - KDP Print US.

Patel, V. (2011). Traditional healers for mental health care in Africa. *Global Health Action*, 4, 10.3402/ gha.v4i0.7956. 10.3402/gha.v4i0.7956. (accessed 6 March 2023).

Prusak, J. (2016). Differential diagnosis of "religious or spiritual problem" – possibilities and limitations implied by the V-code 62.89 in DSM-5. *Psychiatric Polska (Polish Psychiatry)*, 50(1), 175–186, 10.12740/ PP/59115

Rahman, A. R. (2014). Jinn possession in mental health disorder. [Paper presented at the Jinn and Sihr in Medicine: Regional Forum organized by Research

Group] LRGS/TD/2012/USM-UKM/KT/03 in colla-boration with GAPPIMA and PISANG, UKM Malaysia. www.pisang.uk/images/files/jinn%20possess ion%20in%20mental%20health%20disorder.pdf (ac-cessed 8 March 2023).

Rahman, H. A., & Hussein, S. (2021). Case study of using *ruqyah* complementary therapy on a British Muslim patient with cluster headache. *European Journal of Medical and Health Sciences,* 3(1). doi: 10.24018/ejmed.2021.3.1.635

Rassool, G. Hussein. (2019). *Evil eye, jinn possession, and mental health issues: An Islāmic perspective* (1st Ed.). Routledge. 10.4324/9781315623764

Rayan, A. (2018). *Ruqyah: Islāmic exorcism.* CreateSpace Independent Publishing Platform.

Ummah Welfare Trust. (2019). *Ruqyah* a remedy for illness, evil eye, magic and jinn from the Quran and Sunnah (2nd Ed.). https://uwt.org/wp-content/uploads/2019/03/Ruqyah-Booklet.pdf (accessed 25 July 2023).

Yusuf, M. S. (2022). Case study of the use of Qur'ān verses as a media for healing disease or *ruqyah* by santri ponpes tahfidz Al-Fatah Pekalongan. 10.31219/osf.io/6yex9

6 Prophetic medicine (*tibb-an-nabawi*) and its relevance to therapeutic practice

Introduction

Prophetic medicine also known as *tibb-an-nabawi* encompasses a wide range of medicinal practices, spiritual modalities, and their applications. It is based on the teachings and actions of the Prophet Muhammad (ﷺ) concerning diseases, their treatments, and patient care (Bhika & Dockrat, 2015). This field of medicine extends to both physical and mental health and offers universal guidelines for patients in all circumstances. It includes preventive measures, curative remedies, mental well-being, and spiritual healing. A unique aspect of *tibb-an-nabawi* is its integration of the body, heart, and soul, promoting a holistic approach to addressing ill health (Bhika & Saville, 2014).

In particular, *tibb-an-nabawi* comprises of:

- The medical and health-related recommendations of the Prophet (ﷺ).
- The treatments that the Prophet (ﷺ) practiced on himself and others.

DOI: 10.4324/9781003344827-6

- The treatments administered to the Prophet (ﷺ) by others with his approval.
- The treatments observed by the Prophet (ﷺ) without any objection on his part.
- The treatments known or heard of by the Prophet (ﷺ) which he did not forbid (Bhika & Dockrat, 2015).

Muhammad Nazzar al-Daqr defines the medicine of the Prophet (ﷺ) as "the science which combines all that has come to us from the Messenger of Alláh (ﷺ) related to the subject of medicine. This would include the verses of the Qur'ân, the blessed Prophetic traditions and will also include the pre-scriptions of the Prophet (ﷺ) as he administered treatment to some of his companions, when they asked him for cures, or when he instructed them in some remedy. Likewise, this definition encompasses the advice which concerns the healthy living of a human being pertaining to his food and drink, his dwelling and marriage. It also covers the injunctions related to medicine and medication, the etiquettes to be observed and the legal responsibilities of the practitioner" (Bhika & Dockrat, 2015, pp. 20–21).

According to Ibn Al-Qayyim Al-Jawziyyah in his famous book *Medicine of the Prophet*, the science of medicine consists of three basic rules. This includes preserving good health, avoiding what might cause harm, and ridding the body of harmful substances. Prophetic medicine has a divine element to it which sets it apart from all other forms of conventional medicine. It is based on divine revelation from Alláh to His Messenger (ﷺ) and as such holds a superior position as a recommended remedy (Al-Jawziyyah, 2010). This category of foods and medicine has been commended in the Qur'ân and *hadīth* and has been shown to have several health advantages. In his book, Zaad Al Ma'ad, Ibn Al-Qayyim Al-Jawziyyah, said: "The medication of the Messenger (ﷺ), is not identical to the medicine of physicians." "While others' medicine is inductive, assumptive, and experimental, the medicine of the Prophet (ﷺ) is definite, categorical, and Godly medicine, given by the revelation, Prophethood niche, and sagacity" (cited in Iqbal et al., 2021, p. 368). He further states that comparing scientific knowledge to revelation would be the same as comparing the rest of the sciences to what was revealed to the Prophet (ﷺ). It is not surprising that the Prophet (ﷺ) provided us with a type of medicine that current-day doctors are yet to understand, although we find much current research which confirms what the Prophet (ﷺ) suggested some 1,400 years ago (Al-Jawziyyah, 2010).

Spiritual well-being

The Prophet (ﷺ) mentioned in an authentic narration that within the human body, there is a piece of flesh that, if healthy, makes the entire body sound, but if corrupted, it affects the whole body negatively. This piece of flesh is referred to as the heart (Bukhari (a)). In Prophetic remedies, specific prescriptions are provided to address "diseases of the heart." These remedies aim to strengthen the heart and foster a stronger reliance and dependence on

Alláh. Prophetic medicine places significant emphasis on spiritual well-being, encouraging actions like repentance, seeking forgiveness from Alláh, showing kindness to His creation, and helping those in need. Across generations of Muslims, these prescriptions have been tried and proven to provide a type of cure that conventional doctors and allopathic medication may not fully achieve (Ibn Qayyim Al-Jawziyyah, 2010).

The focus on spiritual well-being in Prophetic medicine is crucial because, when the soul and heart become spiritually stronger, the body becomes more resilient in overcoming illnesses (Al-Jawziyyah, 2010). As Muslims, it is essential not to overlook the role spiritual health plays in our lives. The most effective remedy for ailments that affect the heart and soul lies in drawing closer to Alláh, submitting to Him, remembering Him, and seeking His assistance. The Prophet (ﷺ) has conveyed to us that Alláh has not allowed any disease to exist without also providing its cure. Whoever is aware of the cure can benefit from it, and whoever is unaware of it remains uninformed about the means of healing (Ibn Majah (a)). In another narration, the Prophet (ﷺ) stated that every illness indeed has a cure, and when the appropriate remedy is applied to the disease, it will be brought to an end by the will of Alláh (Muslim (a)).

These narrations emphasise the belief in divine wisdom and mercy, affirming that Alláh, in His infinite knowledge, has not left humanity helpless in the face of illnesses. Instead, He has provided cures and treatments for various ailments. It is upon people to seek knowledge and understanding of these remedies to alleviate suffering and promote good health. These Prophetic teachings encourage the pursuit of medical knowledge and the proper application of remedies, aligning with the principle of using all available means to maintain well-being and seek healing through Alláh's blessings (Bhika & Dockrat, 2015).

According to Ibn Al-Qayyim Al-Jawziyyah, the Prophet's (☙) statement regarding a cure for every disease may refer to both curable and incurable diseases, or it might specifically pertain to curable diseases, and only Alláh knows the absolute truth. The implication of these narrations is that when the appropriate remedy is applied to a sickness, the illness comes to an end. This indicates that there is indeed a remedy for every ailment. The Messenger (☙) has conveyed that when the right treatment is combined with the disease, the result will be recovery. However, it is essential to use the correct dosage and appropriate remedy, as using too much of a remedy may lead to another illness, and using too little may not suffice to cure the disease. Additionally, the timing of the treatment and the body's receptiveness to the prescribed application play a crucial role in the effectiveness of the cure. Hence, when all these circumstances align favourably, the properly applied remedy will be effective in bringing about a cure. Ibn Al-Qayyim Al-Jawziyyah asserts that this interpretation provides the most comprehensive explanation for the narrations regarding diseases and their cures (Al-Jawziyyah, 2010).

These authentic narrations highlight the importance for Muslims to seek and apply appropriate medicines and remedies when dealing with illnesses. This practice of seeking treatment does not contradict the concept of dependence on Alláh. On the contrary, it is in line with the belief in the Oneness of Alláh (*tawheed*), which requires responding to harmful elements in a manner and method that Alláh has provided for us (LifewithAlláh, 2023). Refraining from using available remedies would be contradictory to reliance on Alláh and going against the teachings of the Prophet (爨) (Al-Jawziyyah, 2010). Abandoning medical treatments in the name of excessive reliance on Alláh would weaken our reliance (*tawakkul*) because it disregards the means that Alláh has provided to alleviate suffering and find healing. This would not be true reliance, but rather an act of foolishness and ignorance instead of true *tawakkul* (LifewithAlláh, 2023; Al-Jawziyyah, 2010).

Moreover, these narrations refute the notion held by some individuals that seeking medical treatment is unnecessary, and if recovery is destined, it will happen without the need for medicine. This belief is incorrect, as it neglects the wisdom of Alláh, who has created remedies for various diseases. Alláh's decree and destiny do not negate the obligation to seek medical help and use available treatments as means of healing (Bhika & Dockrat, 2015; Al-Jawziyyah cited in Islām Q&A, 1999a). The Prophet (爨) has said, "Alláh has sent down the disease and the cure and has made for every disease the cure. So, treat sickness, but do not use anything haram" (Abu Dawud (a)). In summary, Muslims are encouraged to seek medical treatments and remedies while maintaining trust and reliance on Alláh, recognising that the use of these remedies is part of Alláh's divine plan for maintaining health and seeking recovery. To help us answer this question, we can refer to another explanation by the Prophet (ﷺ) Abu Khuzamah: "I said, 'O Messenger of Alláh, the *ruqyah* (divine remedies – Islāmic supplication formula) that we use, the medicine we take and the prevention we seek, does all this change Alláh's appointed destiny? He said, 'They are in fact a part of Alláh's appointed destiny'" (Ibn Majah (b)).

Indeed, there are significant differences between conventional medicine and *tibb-an-nabawi* in their underlying philosophies and approaches to health and medicine. Conventional medicine primarily focuses on the physical aspects of health and healing, relying on scientific evidence and measurable data. It often disregards explanations that extend beyond the physical realm, such as spiritual or metaphysical factors. The philosophy of conventional medicine tends to adhere to the principle of, if we cannot measure it, then it does not exist, emphasising empirical evidence and objective measurements in diagnosis and treatment (Bhika, 2018; Bhika & Dockrat, 2015). In contrast, *tibb-an-nabawi* encompasses a more holistic approach to health and healing. It not only addresses the physical aspect of diseases but also considers spiritual, mental, and emotional well-being. Prophetic medicine recognises the interconnectedness of the body, heart, and soul and emphasises the importance of maintaining balance in all these aspects to achieve overall well-being (Bhika & Dockrat, 2015; Bhika & Saville, 2014; Al-Jawziyyah, 2010).

Conventional medicine often views the human body as a mechanistic system, seeing health and illness as outcomes of interactions between the body's various components and substructures. In this model, the focus is on identifying and treating specific physical ailments (Bhika, 2018). On the other hand, *tibb-an-nabawi* views health and illness in a broader context, taking into account not just physical symptoms but also the spiritual and mental aspects of a person's health. Prophetic medicine places a strong emphasis on preventive measures, natural remedies, and the role of spirituality in promoting healing and overall well-being. These fundamental differences between conventional medicine and *tibb-an-nabawi* result in distinct interpretations of health and different approaches to medicine, with each system offering its unique benefits and limitations (Bhika, 2018; Bhika & Dockrat, 2015). The World Health Organisation (WHO) defines health as "A state of complete physical, mental and social well-being and not merely the absence of disease" (World Health Organisation, n.d). This definition disregards the emotional and more importantly the spiritual aspects especially in the case of a Muslim patient. A Muslim's understanding of the makeup of a human being is a combination of body and soul. *Tibb-an nabawi* emphasises the importance of maintaining a healthy body, spiritual heart, and a healthy soul and provides guidance for both physical and spiritual health, the latter which includes emotional well-being (Bhika & Dockrat, 2015). The practice of *tibb-an-nabawi* therefore not only focuses on treatment after illness or the absence of disease but also places equal emphasis on preserving health.

In this section, we will focus on specific remedies and modalities from *tibb-an-nabawi* that have been found to offer significant benefits in treating psychological ailments and concerns when used as part of a holistic approach. These remedies are based on practical experience and previous studies, and their application has shown positive results. Table 6.1 presents the selected remedies and their potential benefits for psychological health. These remedies, when used in conjunction with a holistic approach that includes spiritual practices, healthy lifestyle choices, and appropriate professional support, can contribute to improving psychological well-being.

Table 6.1 Selected remedies and their potential benefits for psychological health

Selected remedies	Benefits for psychological health
Talbina	A type of barley porridge recommended by the Prophet (ﷺ) for various ailments, including sadness and grief. It is known to have soothing and comforting effects on the mind and emotions.
Honey	Honey is praised in Prophetic traditions for its various healing

(Continued)

Table 6.1 (Continued)

Selected remedies	Benefits for psychological health
	properties. It can be beneficial for relaxation, improving sleep, and reducing anxiety.
Black seed (*Nigella sativa*)	Black seed is a well-known Prophetic remedy with numerous health benefits, including its potential to alleviate stress and anxiety.
Zamzam water	Zamzam water is considered blessed and has a spiritually uplifting quality. It is used for its healing properties and has calming effects on the mind and soul.
Olive oil	Olive oil is mentioned in the Qur'ân and *Hadīths* for its numerous health benefits. Its consumption is believed to improve overall well-being, including emotional health.
Cupping therapy (*hijama*)	A therapeutic method endorsed by the Prophet (ﷺ). Hijama is thought to release emotional blockages and improve blood flow, which can positively impact mental and emotional health.
Senna and sanoot	Herbal remedies known for their benefits in improving digestive health, which can have a direct effect on emotional well-being (Al-Jawziyyah, 2010).

Talbina

Indeed, talbina is a traditional barley dish cooked with milk and sometimes sweetened with honey. From a Prophetic perspective, the consumption of talbina is recommended, especially during times of sadness or distress, due to its beneficial effects on soothing hearts and relieving sadness (Badrasawi, et al., 2013). The Prophet (صلى الله عليه وسلم) himself recommended talbina and attested to its positive effects on emotional well-being. He said, "It (talbina) strengthens the heart of the bereaved person and removes some of the sorrow within the heart of the ill person, similar to how one of you removes dust from their face by washing their face with water" (Ibn Majah (c)). This Prophetic guidance highlights the potential comforting and therapeutic properties of talbina, making it a recommended remedy for those experiencing grief or sadness. The combination of barley, milk, and honey in talbina may offer a nourishing and soothing effect, which can have a positive impact on one's emotional state. The narration from Aisha (May Alláh be pleased with her) provides a practical example of how talbina was used in Prophetic medicine to address emotional distress and grief. Whenever one of her relatives passed away, Aisha (May Alláh be pleased with her) would gather women, and she would prepare a pot of talbina. She would then mix the talbina with tharid, a dish prepared from meat and bread. Aisha (May Alláh be pleased with her) would encourage the women to eat it, as she had heard the Prophet (صلى الله عليه وسلم) saying that talbina soothes the heart of the patient and relieves some of their sadness (Bukhari (b)). In this context, Aisha (May Alláh be pleased with her) recognised the importance of addressing the emotional needs of those who were grieving. She understood that grief could have a significant impact on a person's well-being, and by preparing the talbina, she provided them with a comforting and nourishing remedy to help alleviate their sadness (Awaad et al., 2021).

It is worth noting that modern research has also explored the potential benefits of talbina and other Prophetic foods in managing emotional distress. As mentioned, talbina was used by Aisha (May Alláh be pleased with her) to treat anxiety and grief-induced psychosis. This indicates that these traditional remedies have been valued for their potential therapeutic effects on emotional well-being for centuries (Awaad et al., 2021). The clinical trial conducted by Badarsawi et al. (2013) demonstrates the potential benefits of talbina as a complementary treatment for mood and depression among elderly individuals who had been institutionalised. The study included 30 depressed elderly subjects, and assessments were made using various scales to measure mood, depression, stress, and anxiety at different time points. The results of the intervention revealed significant positive effects of talbina on reducing depression and enhancing mood among the patients. This indicates that talbina can be a useful addition to a holistic treatment plan for patients facing challenges related to grief due to the loss of loved ones, as well as for those experiencing anxiety and depression. The findings from this clinical trial align with the Prophetic tradition and the wisdom of Aisha (May Alláh be pleased with her) who recognised the soothing effects of talbina on the heart and emotions. It reinforces the value of Prophetic foods like talbina as potential remedies for promoting emotional well-being.

Honey (*asal*)

Honey is known to be used as an antidote and is beneficial for human consumption and is used as a sweetener in many foods and drinks. It has been commonly used by the Greeks, Egyptians, Chinese, and Indians for its notable medicinal value. Honey is composed of fructose, glucose, iron, calcium, phosphate, sodium, chlorine, potassium, and magnesium as well as some amounts of undetermined elements (Purbrafani et al., 2014). More than 1,400 years ago Alláh and His Messenger (ﷺ) informed us that honey has a variety of healing properties. Honey is mentioned in the Qur'ân and described as a source of healing:

وَأَوْحَىٰ رَبُّكَ إِلَى ٱلنَّحْلِ أَنِ ٱتَّخِذِي مِنَ ٱلْجِبَالِ بُيُوتًا وَمِنَ ٱلشَّجَرِ وَمِمَّا يَعْرِشُونَ ثُمَّ كُلِي مِن كُلِّ ٱلثَّمَرَٰتِ فَٱسْلُكِي سُبُلَ رَبِّكِ ذُلُلًا يَخْرُجُ مِنْ بُطُونِهَا شَرَابٌ مُّخْتَلِفٌ أَلْوَٰنُهُ فِيهِ شِفَاءٌ لِّلنَّاسِ إِنَّ فِي ذَٰلِكَ لَآيَةً لِّقَوْمٍ يَتَفَكَّرُونَ

- *And the Lord inspired the bee, saying, take your habitations in the mountains and in the trees and in what they erect. Then, eat all fruits and follow the ways of your Lord made easy (for you)'. There comes forth from their bellies a drink of varying colours wherein is healing for men. Verily in this is indeed a sign for people who think.* (An-Nahl 16: 68,69, interpretation of the meaning)

Furthermore, a narration by the Prophet (☙) states that "There is healing in three: a cupping operation, a drink of honey, and cauterisation with fire, but I forbid my nation from using cauterisation" (Bukhari, (c)) as cited in Abuaminaelias, Elias, 2014). As can be seen from the above, honey is highlighted both in the Qur'ân and the authentic *hadīth* as a recommended remedy and a means for healing. A study conducted by British researchers in 2009 investigated the impact of honey and saffron supplementation on cognitive function in 212 patients with dementia. After an eight-week treatment period, the patients showed noteworthy enhancement in their sleep and memory patterns. The study also suggested that longer-term treatment, even up to two years, could lead to further improvement in the recovery rate (Hosseinzadeh et al., 2004). In a study conducted by Sheas et al. (2019), honey was demonstrated to be an effective remedy against depression, attributed to its antioxidant properties. The presence of polyphenols in honey was found to be beneficial for both the treatment and management of depressive disorders. Furthermore, more recent research has revealed that the polyphenols in honey play significant roles in combating various neurological disorders, including Alzheimer's disease, Parkinson's disease, Huntington's disease, and depression (Iftikhar et al., 2022). In another study by Adeniyi et al. (2023), honey was found to effectively ameliorate poor cognitive performance, anxiety, motor coordination responses to neuroinflammation, and oxidative stress induced by lipopolysaccharide (LPS). These studies collectively highlight the potential therapeutic effects of honey in addressing cognitive and neurological conditions, as well as its role in promoting emotional well-being and combating depression. The presence of polyphenols and antioxidant properties in honey may contribute to its beneficial effects on various aspects of brain health.

As Muslims in helping professions, it is essential to recognise the value of divine prescriptions, such as honey, as part of a holistic approach to therapeutic incorporation. Mental health challenges should not be disregarded when considering such remedies, as evidenced by the studies mentioned above. These studies have shown the potential benefits of honey in addressing neurological and psychological conditions. In conjunction with psychotherapy and medication, honey can be prescribed for daily consumption as part of a comprehensive treatment plan for patients presenting with neurological and psychological challenges. The antioxidant properties and polyphenols present in honey may contribute to its potential therapeutic effects in improving cognitive function, reducing anxiety, and alleviating symptoms of depression. However, it is crucial to remember that honey should not be viewed as a standalone treatment for mental health conditions. Instead, it should be used as a complementary component in combination with evidence-based interventions and professional mental health care.

Black seed (*habatus sawda*)

The Prophet (☸) said, "In black seed there is healing for every disease, except the saam, saam means death" (Ibn Majah (d)). For thousands of years, plants and herbs have been an important source of both nutrition and medicine. Throughout history, the black seed has been used for its nutritive, preventative, and curative effects (Hoosen, n.d). In countries throughout the world, there is evidence of its usage in the treatment of a many differing ailments. In the Greco-Arab/Unani-Tibb systems of medicine, which finds its origin with the Greek philosophers Hippocrates and Galen, thereafter, further conceptualised by the 10th-century Persian physician Ibn Sina (Avicenna), the black seed is considered a valuable remedy and stimulant in a variety of conditions (Hoosen, n.d). In his book, "The Canon of Medicine," Ibn Sina has recommended the use of black seeds for enhancement of the body's energy and as support during recovery from fatigue and dispiritedness. The black seed is highly rich and diverse in its composition, containing amino acids, proteins, carbohydrates, and fixed and volatile oils (Khan, 1999; Muhtasib et al., 2005). Among the promising medicinal plants, black seed has shown potential in managing depression and other neurological disorders (Perveen et al., 2014; Yimer et al., 2019). The evidence suggests that black seed can yield positive outcomes as part of therapeutic interventions, even for mental health challenges like depression. Taking into account the authentic *hadīth*, which states that black seed is a cure for all ailments except death, Muslim practitioners should adopt an assertive stance regarding the therapeutic benefits of incorporating black seed as part of their clients' treatment plans. These findings highlight the potential of black seed as a natural remedy with diverse medicinal properties, and its integration into therapeutic interventions can be considered as a complementary approach in managing mental health challenges.

ZamZam water

The well of *ZamZam* is believed to have first appeared around 5,000 years ago when the Prophet Ismaeel (May Alláh be pleased with him) and his mother Hajar were in desperate need of water. Hajar ran between the hills of Safa and Marwah seven times in search of water to save her son, and miraculously, the well of *ZamZam* sprang under the feet of Ismaeel (May Alláh be pleased with him). *ZamZam* water is known for its purity, as it contains no moss, insects, fungus, or any other impurities (Stagnaro, 2011). Additionally, it has a higher level of natural minerals compared to average desalinated water. In recent times, biophysical semeiotics experiments have provided new evidence suggesting a potential connection between water, memory, and healing information. These experiments build upon Emoto's hypothesis, which explores changes to water crystals achieved by exposing water to music and songs (Stagnaro & Caramel, 2011a and 2011b; Stagnaro, 2011). The association of *ZamZam* water with the concept of water memory and its potential healing properties is a topic of interest and further research in the field of biophysics. However, it is essential to approach such claims with scientific rigour and continue exploring the potential therapeutic effects of *ZamZam* water through rigorous scientific studies (Stagnaro, 2011).

In his research, Emoto (2004) investigated the response of *ZamZam* water to different sound frequencies. He found that this water had a unique interaction and reaction when the words of Alláh were recited upon it. Emoto (2004) conducted an experiment using a few drops of *ZamZam* water and recited the Arabic phrase *Bismillah* (in the name of Alláh, the Beneficent, and Most Merciful) into the water. He observed a distinctive arrangement of water particles, forming a unique shape compared to water particles from other regions around the world. Interestingly, Emoto (2004) noticed that even after diluting the *ZamZam* water 1,000 times, he was unable to crystallise it. However, upon freezing the water, he obtained a uniquely shaped crystal.

The Messenger (ﷺ) said, "The best water on the face of the earth is the water of ZamZam; it is a kind of food and a healing from sickness" (al-Jaami cited in Islām Q&A, 1998b)). Ibn Abbas reported that Prophet (ﷺ) said, "The water of *ZamZam* is good for whatever is drunk for (whatever one intends while drinking it)" (Ibn Majah (e)). This last *hadīth* is of particular importance for the mental health practitioner and their client. From it, we realise that irrespective of what the client presents with, *ZamZam* would always be a beneficial remedy. The key lies in the intention for which it is drunk. The practitioner would provide the necessary psycho-spiritual education in relation to the use of *ZamZam* as a remedy for their presenting concern. If the client drinks the *ZamZam* with the intention of relief from anxiety, for example, this would serve as a valid prescription based on divine revelation.

Sunnah cupping (*hijama*)

Hijama, also known as *Sunnah* cupping, has been used since the time of the Prophet Muhammad (ﷺ). The Prophet (ﷺ) himself received cupping therapy for various ailments and placed great emphasis on its use as a treatment. Wet cupping therapy, which is commonly referred to as "blood-letting," is a practice of Arabic origin (Furhad & Bokhari, 2023). Cupping therapy has a long history and was a popular treatment in Arabic and Islāmic countries. Renowned physicians such as Ibn Sina, Al-Zahrawi, and Abu Bakr Al-Razi recommended its use (Aboushanab & Alsanad, 2018). The process involves creating small scratches in specific parts of the body and applying a vacuum to draw out blood and fluids from these areas. In modern times, glass or plastic suction cups are commonly used for this purpose (Al-Bedah et al., 2019). The primary objective of blood-letting, particularly in the context of cupping therapy or wet cupping, is to remove accumulated chemicals and toxins from the body. Unlike traditional blood donation or venipuncture, blood-letting in cupping therapy involves drawing blood from under the skin through small incisions (Al-Bedah et al., 2019).

Research has indicated that cupping therapy may be an effective method for extracting heavy metals from the body. Studies, such as the one conducted by Umar et al. (2018), have shown that heavy metals like aluminium, lead, mercury, and silver can be found in higher quantities when extracted through cupping therapy compared to traditional venous blood draws. The treatment can be applied to any part of the body, and common application points include the back, head, shoulders, waist, chest, legs, feet, and other body parts depending on the presenting problem. Patients are required to fast for approximately 3 to 4 hours prior to the procedure (Al-Bedah et al., 2019). This is also a recommendation from the *Sunnah*.

The cupping therapy procedure typically begins with the disinfection of the area that will be treated. Suction cups are then applied to the skin to create a vacuum effect. After a certain period, the cups are removed, and the skin is superficially lacerated using a sterile blade or scalpel. The cups are then reapplied to draw out the blood from the incisions. The practitioner allows the bleeding to stop naturally before removing the cups. The incisions are cleaned, and the clotted blood is discarded. To prevent infection, the practitioner may apply black seed oil, raw honey, or any other healing agent to the treated area. Patients are advised not to shower for 12 to 24 hours after the procedure to minimise the risk of infection (Ucun, 2022; Koran & Irbun, 2021).

Islāmically, *hijama* is considered a praiseworthy treatment. The following are authentic narrations from the *Sunnah* that motivate incorporating *hijama* into holistic therapeutic practice. The Prophet (ﷺ) said, "If there is anything good in the medicines with which you treat yourselves, it is in the incision of the cupping therapist, or a drink of honey or cauterisation with fire, but I do not like to be cauterised" (Bukhari (d)). Narrated Jabir bin 'Abdullah who stated that he paid Al-Muqanna a visit during his illness and said, "I will not leave till he gets cupped, for I heard Allāh's Messenger (ﷺ) saying, "There is healing in cupping" (Bukhari (e)). It is narrated in Bukhari and Muslim that Anas ibn Malik was asked about the earnings of the cupping therapist, and he said: The Prophet (ﷺ) was treated with cupping by Abu Taybah. He ordered that he should be given two sa'a of food, and he spoke with his masters so that they reduced what they used to take from his earnings. And he said, "The best medicine with which you treat yourselves is cupping, or it is one of the best of your medicines" (Islām Q&A, 2002 (c)). In another narration Abdullah ibn Mas'ud reported that the Prophet (ﷺ) said, "I did not pass by an angel from the angels on the night journey (*Al Israa wal Me'raaj*) except that they all said to me "upon you is hijama, O Muhammad", and in another narration he said the angels said, "Oh Muhammad, order cupping (*hijama*) among your ummah" (Tirmidhi (a); Ibn Majah (f)). Abu Hurairah reported that the Messenger (ﷺ) said, "Whoever performs cupping (hijama) on the 17th, 19th or 21st day (of the Islāmic, lunar month) then it is a cure for every disease" (Abu Dawud(b)). These *hadīth* emphasise the importance that was placed on receiving cupping as a treatment, so much so that the Prophet (ﷺ) feared it would become compulsory upon his followers to do so.

A recent systematic review conducted by Ucun (2022) aimed to assess the effects of wet cupping on the treatment of mental illness. The studies explored the effects of wet cupping on various mental health conditions, including migraines, metabolic syndrome, smoking addiction, post-traumatic stress disorder, chronic medical diseases, and depression. In all the included studies, wet cupping was reported to be effective in reducing the psychological symptoms associated with these conditions.

The recent studies conducted by Kordafshari et al. (2017), Rahman et al. (2020), and Reza et al. (2021) provide valuable insights into the potential benefits of cupping therapy for mental health and overall quality of life. The study by Kordafshari et al. (2017) demonstrated that cupping therapy had a positive influence on the quality of life in healthy individuals attending traditional Persian medicine clinics in Tehran. In the case of Rahman et al. (2020), their research highlighted the effectiveness of wet cupping in managing cases of moderate depression. The study conducted by Reza et al. (2021) specifically focused on using wet cupping as a psychological therapy in Muslim villages. The findings of this study indicated that cupping therapy had a tendency to be utilised as a psychological therapy and was effective in reducing negative emotions among the participants. It promoted a sense of happiness, comfort, and tranquility, leading to emotional stability among the Muslim adults. These recent studies collectively suggest that incorporating *Sunnah* cupping as part of a holistic approach to therapy may have beneficial impacts on mental health and overall well-being for both Muslim and non-Muslim individuals.

Olive oil

The olive is mentioned several times in the Qur'ân. The beautiful verse in *Surah Nur* is one such example,

اَللَّهُ نُورُ ٱلسَّمَٰوَٰتِ وَٱلۡأَرۡضِ مَثَلُ نُورِهِ كَمِشۡكَوٰةٍ فِيهَا مِصۡبَاحٌ ٱلۡمِصۡبَاحُ فِي زُجَاجَةٍ ٱلزُّجَاجَةُ كَأَنَّهَا كَوۡكَبٌ دُرِّيٌّ يُوقَدُ مِنشَجَرَةٍ مُّبَٰرَكَةٍ زَيۡتُونَةٍ لَّا شَرۡقِيَّةٍ وَلَا غَرۡبِيَّةٍ يَكَادُ زَيۡتُهَا يُضِيٓءُ وَلَوۡ لَمۡ تَمۡسَسۡهُ نَارٌ نُّورٌ عَلَىٰ نُورٍ يَهۡدِي ٱللَّهُ لِنُورِهِ مَن يَشَآءُ وَيَضۡرِبُ ٱللَّهُ ٱلۡأَمۡثَٰلَ لِلنَّاسِ وَٱللَّهُ بِكُلِّ شَيۡءٍ عَلِيمٌ

- *Allâh is the Light of the heavens and the earth. The example of His light is like a niche within which is a lamp, the lamp is within glass, the glass as if it were a pearly [white] star lit from [the oil of] a blessed olive tree, neither of the east nor of the west, whose oil would almost glow even if untouched by fire. Light upon light. Allâh guides to His light whom He wills.*

And Alláh presents examples for the people, and Alláh is Knowing of all things. (Nur, 24: 35, interpretation of the meaning)

Olives and olive oil have been mentioned approximately seven times in the Qur'ân. The Prophet (ﷺ) has also mentioned the olive and its oil in authentic *hadīth*. He (ﷺ) advised that we use olive oil as a food and ointment for it comes from a blessed tree. Olive oil has been consumed since ancient times and is well known for its nutritious fats and as medical remedy in addition to being commonly recognised by many cultures and religious groups as a key ingredient either in ceremonies or as part of consumption and anointing (Ilak Peršuric & Damijanic, 2021). Olive oil is an essential ingredient in many Mediterranean foods and is widely utilised across the globe for its health benefits. The oil is known to have important effects on the human body and has protective effects against an array of pathological conditions. Olive oil has been shown to produce an anxiolytic effect by decreasing brain 5HT synthesis and metabolism. Results of the said study supported the use of olive oil as a food supplementation for mood elevation (Perveen et al., 2013).

Similarly, and more recently, Foshati, Ghanizadeh, and Akhlagi (2022) found beneficial effects of extra virgin olive oil (EVOO) on depression symptoms in patients with severe depression but not in those with mild to moderate depression. Their results suggested that the effects were significant from both statistical and clinical points of view. Mitsukura et al.

(2021) studied the effects of olive oil on human stress levels. Mental stress from harsh working environments can have serious implications for human health, both mentally and physically. Symptoms of stress may include feelings of worthlessness, agitation, anxiety, lethargy, and insomnia, as well as behavioural changes. Olive oil has been known to provide stress-relieving effects both when consumed and through application and inhalation. The researchers examined the effects of ingesting EVOO on mitigating stress caused by desk-work. Statistical analysis showed that the stress levels were lower during the olive oil ingestion experiment compared to no-oil experiment, even after an hour of ingestion (Mitsukura et al., 2021). A preliminary study was performed on blood samples of 23 women diagnosed with fibromyalgia (FM) who consumed 50 ml of organic olive oil daily for three weeks. The findings imply that EVOO may successfully protect women with FM against oxidative stress. Furthermore, it was shown to improve the functional capacity and health-related psychological status among these women (Rus et al., 2017). These findings support the use of olive oil as a valuable source of remedy in people with FM. The above research studies have shown that using EVOO as part of a comprehensive therapeutic plan could prove beneficial for patients presenting with stress anxiety, depression, and FM.

Senna

Senna, a plant with well-known medicinal properties, contains various compounds such as sugar molecules, mucilage tannins, and flavonoids (Khan, 2020). Its commercial use is mainly as a laxative due to its ability to stimulate bowel movements, but it is also believed to offer other health benefits. Emodin, a glycoside found in senna, possesses anti-inflammatory and antispasmodic properties and has demonstrated antiviral activity (Khan, 2020). These compounds contribute to cellular regeneration, detoxification, and cleansing effects in the body. According to Ibn Al-Qayyim Al-Jawziyyah, senna is considered an excellent medicine not only as a laxative but also for relaxing muscles and improving hair texture. It is believed to have positive effects against head lice, headache, rashes, and epilepsy (Al-Jawziyyah, 2010). Although there are no known studies on the use of senna specifically for mental health disturbances, its inclusion in this chapter is based on two significant considerations. First, there is growing recognition of the importance of gut health in relation to both physical and mental well-being, and the Prophet's (ﷺ) advice in this regard is noteworthy. Second, senna is mentioned due to a profound *hadīth* that holds significance in its therapeutic potential. Ibn Majah narrated in book of medicine that the Prophet (ﷺ) said, "you should use senna and the sannut, for in them there is healing for every disease, except the saam." It was said: "O Messenger of Alláh, what is the saam?" He said, "Death." (One of the narrators) 'Amr said, "Ibn Abu 'Ablah said: the 'sannut is dill." Others said, "Rather, it is honey that is kept in a skin (i.e., receptacle) used for ghee" (Ibn Majah (f)). This *hadīth* suggests that using senna as a remedy would be of great benefit for all diseases/ailments including mental health disorders. In recent years, science has proven the connection between the gut and the brain (Clapp et al., 2017; Appleton, 2018; Gądek-Michalska, 2013).

Research has shown that inflammation of the gastro-intestinal tract causes strain on the micro-biome by the release of cytokines and neurotrans-mitters (Clapp et al., 2017). According to Appleton (2018), the gut-brain axis is a bi-directional network of communication that links the enteric and central nervous systems. It is not only anatomical but includes the endocrine, humoral, metabolic, and immune routes of communication. Depressive and anxiety-like disorders are characterised by neuro-plastic and organisational changes, as well as neu-rochemical dysfunction, and the deregulation of these systems is attributed to cytokine release secondary to an exaggerated systemic response to stressors usually resulting in illness (Neufeld et al., 2011; Clapp et al., 2017). The review by Clapp et al. (2017) demonstrated the importance of a healthy microbiome, with special attention to gut micro-biota, for patients suffering from anxiety and depression because dysbiosis and inflammation in the central nervous system have been linked as potential causes of mental illness (Daulatzai, 2015).

The Messenger of Alláh (ﷺ) said, "The son of Adam cannot fill a vessel worse than his stomach, as it is enough for him to take a few bites to straighten his back. If he cannot do it, then he may fill it with a third of his food, a third of his drink, and a third of his breath" (Tirmidhi (b)). Ibn Rajab Al-Hanbali pointed out that this *hadīth* encompasses all medical principles. This advice from the Prophet (ﷺ) is one that highlights the concept of moderation and balance when it comes to eating and filling one's stomach.

Research has indicated that certain diets and eating habits can promote inflammation, which in turn may exacerbate depressive symptoms. This suggests that a diet influencing inflammation may contribute to increased depression, while depression itself can further advance inflammation (Appleton, 2018). Additionally, studies by Eltokhi and Sommer (2022) have shown a strong association between microbiota dysbiosis (imbalance in gut bacteria) and depression. This association could potentially lead to improved diagnostic accuracy and personalised treatment selection for depression. Moreover, modifying the gut microbiota composition through nutritional interventions, prebiotics, or probiotic supplementations could offer a promising future strategy in psychiatry for the treatment and prevention of depression.

Considering the Prophetic narration on senna being an encompassing cure for all ailments except death, and the researched anti-inflammatory and purgative effects of senna, along with its other benefits, senna is included as a prescriptive recommendation for people presenting with depression and other mood disorders. Its potential to address gut health and inflammation aligns with the growing understanding of the gut-brain connection and the role of nutrition in mental health.

Conclusion

The knowledge and wisdom inherited in the Islāmic tradition through divine revelation, particularly

Prophetic medicine or *tibb-an-nabawi*, hold a special place of reverence and importance. Muslims acknowledge and appreciate all permissible medical interventions and treatments that fall outside the realm of divine revelation. The Prophet Muhammad (ﷺ) himself advised seeking cures, and this extends beyond what is specifically mentioned in the Qur'ânic or Prophetic texts. Therefore, while all beneficial and permissible medical interventions are valued, *tibb-an-nabawi* remains highly regarded and is considered superior in comparison to other forms of medical knowledge founded by science.

It is a common tendency for people to prioritise Western approaches and prescriptions when dealing with sickness or health concerns, often relegating Prophetic prescriptions to a secondary or last resort, if considered at all. As Muslim practitioners in the helping profession, it is essential to reconsider this approach. Prophetic remedies should be incorporated into mainstream therapeutic interventions, especially in the field of mental health. The rich tradition of *tibb-an nabawi* offers valuable insights into the holistic approach to health, encompassing physical, mental, and spiritual well-being. By integrating Prophetic remedies into therapeutic interventions, Muslim practitioners can provide a more comprehensive and culturally sensitive approach to mental health care. As with any treatment approach, individualised care, professional judgement, and consideration of the patient's specific needs and beliefs are crucial. By embracing the teachings of *tibb-an nabawi* and incorporating Prophetic remedies into mainstream mental health care, Islāmic psychologists and Muslim practitioners can better serve their clients and contribute to a more inclusive and holistic approach to well-being.

References

AbdurRahman.org (2016). *The talbina gives rest to the heart of the patient and makes it active and relieves some of his sorrow and grief.* https://abdurrahman.org/2014/01/28/talbina/ (accessed 18 March 2023).

Abu Dawud [a]. *Sunan Abu Dawud* 3874. In-book reference: Book 29, Hadīth 20. English translation: Book 28, Hadīth 3865.

Abu Dawud [b]. *Sunan Abu Dawud* 3861. In-book reference: Book 29, Hadīth 7. English translation: Book 28, Hadīth 3852.

Aboushanab, T. S., & AlSanad, S. (2018). Cupping therapy: An overview from a modern medicine perspective. *Journal of Acupuncture and Meridian Studies*, 11(3), 83–87. 10.1016/j.jams.2018.02.001

Adeniyi, I. A., Babalola, K. T., Adekoya, V. A., Oyebanjo, O., Ajayi, A. M., & Onasanwo, S. A. (2023). Neuropharmacological effects of honey in lipopolysaccharide-induced neuroinflammation, cognitive impairment, anxiety and motor impairment. *Nutritional Neuroscience*, 26(6), 511–524. 10.1080/1028415X.2022.2063578

Al-Bedah, A. M. N., Elsubai, I. S., Qureshi, N. A., Aboushanab, T. S., Ali, G. I. M., El-Olemy, A. T., Khalil, A. A. H., Khalil, M. K. M., & Alqaed, M. S. (2019). The medical perspective of cupping therapy: Effects and mechanisms of action. *Journal of Traditional and Complementary Medicine*, 9(2), 90–97. 10.1016/j.jtcme.2018.03.003

Al-Jawziyyah, I. Q. (2010). *Healing with the medicine of the Prophet* (J. A. Rub, Trans). Darussalam, Riyadh: Fordham University USA.

Appleton J. (2018). The gut-brain axis: Influence of microbiota on mood and mental health. Integrative medicine, *Encinitas, Calif*, 17(4), 28–32.

At Tirmidhi [a]. *Jami' at-Tirmidhi* 2052. In-book reference: Book 28, Hadīth 17. English translation: Vol 4, Book 2, 2052.

At Tirmidhi [b]. *Jami' at-Tirmidhi* 2380. In-book reference: Book 36, Hadīth 77. English translation: Vol. 4, Book 10, Hadīth 2380.

Awaad, R., Alsayed, D., & Helal, H. (2021). Holistic healing. Islām's legacy of mental health. The Muslim Reader. *Yaqeen Institute for Islāmic Research*, 57–63.

Badrasawi, M. M., Shahadan, N. H., & Salleh, S. N. (2013). Talbina from an Islāmic perspective: A review of literature. *International Food Research Journal*, 20(4), 1663–1669.

Badrasawi, M. M., Shahar, S., Abd Manaf, Z., & Haron, H. (2013). Effect of talbinah food consumption on depressive symptoms among elderly individuals in long term care facilities, randomized clinical trial. *Clinical Interventions in Aging*, 8, 279–285. 10.2147/CIA.S37586

Bhika, R. (2018). *Theoretical principles of tibb: A treatise on the philosophy, aetiology, pathology, diagnosis and therapeutics from Greek, Arab and Unani Sources.* South Africa: Ibn Sina Institute of Tibb.

Bhika, R., & Dockrat, I. (2015). *Medicine of the prophet Tibb Al-Nabawi your guide to healthy living.* South Africa: Ibn Sina Institute of Tibb.

Bhika, R., & Saville, J. (2014). *Healing with Tibb: A holistic, empowering approach to understanding and managing common illness conditions.* South Africa: Ibn Sina Institute of Tibb.

Bukhari [a]. *Sahih al-Bukhari* 52. In-book reference: Book 2, Hadīth 45, USC-MSA web (English) reference: Vol. 1, Book 2, Hadīth 50.

Bukhari [b]. *Sahih al-Bukhari* 5689. In-book reference: Book 76, Hadīth 12 USC-MSA web (English) reference: Vol. 7, Book 71, Hadīth 593.

Bukhari [c]. *Sahih al-Bukhari* 5704. In-book reference: Book 76, Hadīth 24 USC-MSA web (English) reference: Vol. 7, Book 71, Hadīth 60.

Bukhari [d]. *Sahih al-Bukhari* 5704. In-book reference: Book 76, Hadīth 24 USC-MSA web (English) reference: Vol. 7, Book 71, Hadīth 605.

Bukhari [e]. *Sahih al-Bukhari* 5697. In-book reference: Book 76, Hadīth 19 USC-MSA web (English) reference: Vol. 7, Book 71, Hadīth 600.

Clapp, M., Aurora, N., Herrera, L., Bhatia, M., Wilen, E., & Wakefield, S. (2017). Gut microbiota's effect on mental health: The gut-brain axis. *Clinics and Practice*, 7(4), 987. 10.4081/cp.2017.987

Daulatzai, M. A. (2015). Non-celiac gluten sensitivity triggers gut dysbiosis, neuroinflammation, gut-brain axis dysfunction, and vulnerability for dementia. *CNS and Neurological Disorders,* 14, 110–131.

Eltokhi, A., & Sommer, I. E. (2022). A reciprocal link between gut microbiota, inflammation and depression: A place for probiotics?. *Frontiers in Neuroscience*, 16, 852506. 10.3389/fnins.2022.852506

Elias, A. A. (2014). Hadith on hijama: There is healing in cupping, honey. https://www.abuaminaelias.com/dailyhadithonline/2014/05/06/hijamah-cupping-honey (accessed 21 March 2023).

Elias, A. A. (2021). Abdullah on medicine: Use the Quran and honey for healing. Daily Hadīth Online. https://www.abuaminaelias.com/dailyhadīthonline/2021/04/20/quran-honey/ (accessed 21 January 2023).

Emoto, M. (2004). *Love thyself: Message from water.* Kyoikusha, Tokyo: HADO. 3.50–51.

Foshati, S., Ghanizadeh, A., & Akhlaghi, M. (2022). Extra-virgin olive oil improves depression symptoms without affecting salivary cortisol and brain-derived neurotrophic factor in patients with major depression: A double-blind randomized controlled trial. *Journal of the Academy of Nutrition and Dietetics*, 122(2), 284–297. 10.1016/j.jand.2021.07.016

Furhad, S., & Bokhari, A. A. (2023). *Cupping therapy*. In StatPearls. StatPearls Publishing.

Gądek-Michalska, A., Tadeusz, J. K., Rachwalska, P., & Bugajski, J. (2013). Cytokines, prostaglandins and nitric oxide in the regulation of stress-response systems. *Pharmacological Reports*, 65(6), 1655–1662. 10.1016/S1734-1140(13)71527-5

Hoosen (n.d.). *Black seed: Natures miracle.* https://www. tibb.co.za/articles/black%20seed%20article.pdf (accessed 13 October 2022).

Hosseinzadeh H., Karimi G., & Niapoor M. (2004). Antidepressant effect of Crocus sativus L stigma extracts and their constituents, crocin and safranal, in mice. *Acta* Horticulturae, 650, 435–445.

Ibn Majah [a]. *Sunan Ibn Majah* 3438. In-book reference: Book 31, Hadīth. English translation: Vol 4. Book 31, Hadīth 3438.

Ibn Majah [b]. *Sunan Ibn Majah* 3237. In-book reference: Book 31, Hadīth 2. English translation: Vol 4. Book 31, Hadīth 3437.

Ibn Majah [c]. *Sunan Ibn Majah* 3445. In-book reference: Book 31, Hadīth 10. English translation: Vol 4. Book 31, Hadīth 3445.

Ibn Majah [d]. *Sunan Ibn Majah* 3447. In-book reference: Book 31, Hadīth 12. English translation: Vol. 4, Book 31, Hadīth 344.

Ibn Majah [e]. *Sunan Ibn Majah* 3062. In-book reference: Book 25, Hadīth 181. English translation: Vol 4, Book 25, Hadīth 3062.

Ibn Majah [f]. *Sunan Ibn Majah* 3479. In-book reference: Book 31, Hadīth 44. English translation: Vol. 4, Book 31, Hadīth 3479.

Iftikhar, S. A., Nausheen, R., Muzaffar, H., Naeem, M. A., Farooq, M., Khurshid, M., Almatroudi, A., Alrumaihi, F., Allemailem, K. S., & Anwar, H. (2022).

Potential therapeutic benefits of honey in neurological disorders: The Role of polyphenols. *Molecules*, 27(10). 10.3390/molecules27103297

Ilak Peršurić, A. S., & Težak Damijanić, A. (2021). Connections between healthy behaviour, perception of olive oil health benefits, and olive oil consumption motives. *Sustainability*, 13(14), 7630. 10.3390/su1314 7630

Iqbal, A. S., Jan, M., Muflih, B., & Jaswir, I. (2021). The role of prophetic food in the prevention and cure of chronic diseases: A review of literature. *Malaysian Journal of Social Sciences and Humanities*, 6(11), 366–375. 10.47405/mjssh.v6i11.1144

Islām Q&A. (1999). '*Do Muslims have to seek medical treatment.*' Islām Question and Answer. Online at: https://Islāmqa.info/en/answers/2438 (accessed 7 July 2023).

Islam Q&A. (1998). '*Merits of Zam Zam water. Islam Question and Answer.*' Online at: https://islamqa.info/en/answers/1698 (accessed 8 July 2023).

Islām Q&A. (1998). '*What are the benefits of Zamzam Water.*' Islām Question and Answer. Online at: https://Islāmqa.info/en/answers/6831 (accessed 15 August 2023).

Islām Q&A. (2002). '*Cupping in Islām: Virtues and benefits*'. Islām Question and Answer. Online at: https://Islāmqa.info/en/answers/21406 (accessed 21 March 2023).

Khan, M. A. (1999). Chemical composition and medicinal properties of Nigella sativa. *Inflammopharmacology*, 7,15–35.

Khan, M. S. A. (2020). A review on senna: An excellent Prophetic herbal medicine. *World Journal of Pharmaceutical and Medical Research*, 6(7), 113–118.

Koran, S., & Irban, A. (2021). Analytical approach to the literature of cupping therapy. *Journal of Korean Society of Physical Medicine*, 16, 1–14. 10.13066/kspm.2021.16.3.1

Kordafshari, G., Ardakani, M. R. S., Keshavarz, M., Esfahani, M. M., Nazem, I., Moghimi, M., Zargaran, A., & Kenari, H. M. (2017). Cupping therapy can improve the quality of life of healthy people in Tehran. *Journal of Traditional Chinese Medicine*, 37(4), 558–562, 10.1016/S0254-6272(17)30164-4

Life with Alláh. (2023). Dhikr and dua. Life with Alláh. https://lifewithAlláh.com/articles/ruqyah/what-is-ruqyah (accessed 20 April 2023).

Mitsukura, Y., Sumali, B., Nara, R., Watanabe, K., Inoue, M., Ishida, K., Nishiwaki, M., & Mimura, M. (2021). Evaluation of olive oil effects on human stress response by measuring cerebral blood flow. *Food Science Nutrition*, 9(4):1851–1859. doi: 10.1002/fsn3. 2099. PMID: 33841804.

Muhtasib, H. G., Najjar, N. E., & Scheider-stock, R.. (2005). The medicinal potential of black seed (Nigella sativa) and its components. *Advances in Phytomedicine*, 2, 133–153. doi:10.1016/S1572-557X(05)02008-8

Muslim. *Sahih Muslim*(a). Mishkat al-Masabih 4515. In-book reference: Book 23, Hadīth 2.

Neufeld, K. A., Kang, N., Bienenstock, J., & Foster, J. A. (2011). Effects of intestinal microbiota on anxiety-like behavior. *Communicative & Integrative Biology*, 4(4), 492–494. 10.4161/cib.4.4.15702

Perveen, T., Haider, S., Zuberi, N. A., Saleem, S., Sadaf, S., & Batool, Z. (2014). Increased 5-HT levels following repeated administration of Nigella sativa L. (black seed) oil produce antidepressant effects in rats. *Scientia Pharmaceutica*, 82(1), 161–170.

Perveen, T., Hashmi, B. M., Haider, S., Tabassum, S., Saleem, S., & Siddiqui, M. A. (2013). Role of monoaminergic system in the etiology of olive oil induced antidepressant and anxiolytic effects in rats. *ISRN Pharmacology*, 10. 10.1155/2013/615685

Purbrafani, A. et al. (2014). The benefits of honey in holy Quran. *International Journal of Pediatrics*, 2(9), 67–73.

Rahman, Z., Akhtar, S., Siddiqui, M. N. M., & Ahmad, G. (2020). Efficacy of wet cupping in the management of depression: A pilot study. *European Journal of Pharmaceutical and Medical Research*, 7(6), 655–657.

Reza, I. F., Utamib, A., Candrac, D., Purwantod, E., Zainuddine, I. A., Altyf, N. N., Apriyantig, N., & Anzila, O. F. (2021). Cupping as a psychological therapy for Muslim in the perspective of Islāmic psychology. *Proceedings of The 4th International Conference of Genuine Psychology*, 202–208.

Rus, A., Molina, F., Ramos, M. M., Martínez-Ramírez, M. J., & del Moral, M. L., (2017). Extra virgin olive oil improves oxidative stress, functional capacity, and health-related psychological status in patients with fibromyalgia: A preliminary study. *Biological Research For Nursing*, 19(1), 106–115. 10.1177/1099800416659370

Sheas, R. A., et al. (2019). Honey as an effective prescription against depression. *Journal of Nutritional Therapeutics*, 8(3), 129–136.

Sheas, M. N., Rasool, H., Rafique, M. N., Tariq, M. R., Muhammad, A., Ali, K. (2019). Exploring the potential of honey and curcumin as antidepressent. *Journal of Zoology. Punjab University*. 34, 89–95.

Stagnaro, S. (2011). Quantum biophysical semeiotics evidences of water-memory-information by means of music energizing action: Caramel's experiment. *Journal of Quantum Biophysical Semeiotics.*

Stagnaro, S., & Caramel, S. (2011a). Two prayer experiment: The effectiveness of different kinds of prayers through QBS assessment. *Journal of Quantum Biophysical Semeiotics.*

Stagnaro, S., & Caramel, S. (2011b). A new way of therapy based on water memory-information: The quantum biophysical approach. *JOQBS.*

Ucun, Y. (2022). Wet cupping (al-hijama) for mental health: A systematic review. *Journal of Acupuncture Research*. Korean Acupuncture and Moxibustion Medicine Society. 10.13045/jar.2022.00031

Umar, N. K., Tursunbadalov, S., Surgun, S., Welcome, M. O., & Dane, S. (2018). The effects of wet cupping therapy on the blood levels of some heavy metals: A pilot study. *Journal Acupuncture and Meridian Studies*, 11(6), 375–379. 10.1016/j.jams.2018.06.005

Yimer, E. M., Tuem, K. B., Karim, A., Ur-Rehman, N., & Anwar, F. (2019). Nigella sativa L. (black cumin): A promising natural remedy for wide range of illnesses. *Evidence-Based Complementary and Alternative Medicine*. 10.1155/2019/1528635.

World Health Organization (n.d). Health and Well-Being. https://www.who.int/data/gho/data/major-themes/health-and-well-being (accessed 17 March 2023).

7 The Islāmic psychotherapist and mental health practitioner
Moving towards a holistic approach

Introduction

There has been a growing global recognition of mental health issues among various racial, religious, and ethnic groups of Muslim communities. This has led to a noticeable trend in adapting counselling and psychotherapeutic approaches that align better with the religious worldview and orientations of Muslim clients. Psychologists, psychotherapists, and counsellors widely agree that mental health problems often manifest as complex issues involving multiple layers and a convergence of psychological, physiological, spiritual, and other imbalances (Joshanloo, 2013; Rassool, 2019). Muslim psychotherapists and counsellors who practice within mainstream Western paradigms and orientations have observed the necessity for a distinct shift within their communities towards integrating faith-based practices into therapeutic interventions. It is crucial to acknowledge that therapists and clients alike recognise that certain Western approaches or treatment plans may contradict fundamental Islāmic principles (Rassool, 2016).

DOI: 10.4324/9781003344827-7

This chapter addresses the role of Islāmic psychothera-pists and mental health practitioners in adopting a comprehensive approach to healing and well-being. This chapter aims to examine the role and responsibil-ities of the Islāmic psychotherapists and mental health practitioners within the holistic paradigm of thera-peutic interventions and to comprehend the Muslim client thoroughly when considering assessment, diag-nosis, and treatment, as this understanding ensures culturally sensitive and effective approaches.

Integrating Islāmic spiritual interventions in mental health treatment

Muslim psychologists, psychotherapists, counsellors, and medical practitioners should recognise that certain mental health issues experienced by Muslim clients may extend beyond the scope of traditional psychological methods and approaches. It is crucial for Muslim practitioners to acknowledge and explore the positive and significant contributions that spiri-tual interventions grounded in Islāmic jurisprudence (*Shar'iah*) can offer in terms of prevention, treatment, and recovery (Al Jeraisy, n.d.). The Islāmic spiritual tradition encompasses various practices and beliefs that can be examined and utilised for therapeutic purposes. It views hardships and adversities as opportunities for developing absolute reliance on Allāh, submitting to Him, and cultivating virtue (Abdussalam Bali, 2015). It is essential to recognise the profound psychological insights embedded within our tradition and extract this timeless guidance for the benefit of all (Al Jeraisy, n.d.).

Regrettably, there is another perspective to consider. Within the Muslim community, there are individuals, including Islāmic psychotherapists, psychiatrists, and medical and mental health practitioners, as well as clients, who do not recognise the importance or may even disregard and overlook the utilisation of Islāmic healing modalities as part of their therapeutic approach (Hecker & Kottler, 2002a; Al-Jeraisy, n.d.). However, proponents of Islāmic and Prophetic healing, who have studied and comprehended these practices, advocate for the integration of such modalities into treatment methods due to the significant benefits they offer in terms of healing both physical and non-physical ailments or afflictions (Al Jeraisy, n.d.). The *Shar'iah* encompasses both religious and secular obligations and may include penalties for transgressions. Within this perspective, the *Shar'iah* affirms the permissibility of seeking healing and treatment through Qur'ānic recitations, Prophetic prayers, and the use of medicine (Al Jeraisy, n.d.).

Allāh says:

وَنُنَزِّلُ مِنَ ٱلْقُرْءَانِ مَا هُوَ شِفَآءٌ وَرَحْمَةٌ لِّلْمُؤْمِنِينَ وَلَا يَزِيدُ ٱلظَّٰلِمِينَ إِلَّا خَسَارًا

And We send down of the Qur'ān that which is healing and mercy for the believers, but it does not increase the wrongdoers except in loss.(Al-Isra', 17:82, interpretation of the meaning)

There are differing opinions among scholars regarding the interpretation of this verse. Some suggest that the verse signifies psychological healing, while others believe it implies that the Qur'ān is a remedy for spiritual, psychological, and physical/physiological problems in general (Abdussalam Bali, 2015). Supporting this notion, an authentic *hadīth* narrated by Aisha (May Allāh be pleased with her) states that the Prophet (ﷺ) entered her room while she was performing *ruqyah* on a woman, and he advised her to treat the woman with the Book of Allāh (Ibn Hibban, 1993). This *hadīth* illustrates that the entire Qur'ān is considered a cure and is not limited to specific ailments, but rather serves as a general source of healing from all harm (Bali, 2015). In another authentic *hadīth* Abu Huraira reported that the Prophet (ﷺ) said, "Allāh did not send down any disease but that He also sent down the cure" (Abu Dāwūd (a)). Ibn Al-Qayyim Al-Jawziyyah commented on this *hadīth* and stated that this is generally true for diseases of the heart, spirit, and body, as well as their cures (Al-Jawziyyah, n.d).

The Prophet Muhammad (ﷺ) is reported to have said that a person is upon the way of his close confidant (*khalil*), so each one of you shall be mindful of whom he makes his *khalil* (Abū Dāwūd, 2009). This statement highlights the signifi-cance of internal qualities and aspects of the psychotherapist and Muslim mental healthcare practitioner. The role of these practitioners differs greatly from that of a traditional therapist, who typically maintains a professional distance and where personal life, values, and ethics may be considered irrelevant within the therapeutic relationship (Kershavazi et al., 2020). In contrast, the Islāmic psychotherapists and mental health practitioners offer a shared value system that aligns with their religious values and orientations.

Role and characteristics

There are some commonalities between the role of the mainstream psychotherapist and the role of the Islāmic psychotherapist. There are also significant differences between the Islāmic psychotherapist and conventional psychotherapists and counsellors (Rassool, 2023). According to Rassool (2023), "The most significant differences are the Islāmic understanding of the nature of human beings, the Islāmic worldview, and the incorporation of spirituality into the therapeutic process" (p. 72). Rassool (2023) further suggested that one role of the Islāmic psychotherapist or counsellor that is the antithesis of the role of a conventional psychotherapist is in the giving of advice. In the prevailing perspective, providing advice is often considered a therapeutic mistake with the potential for negative outcomes. Nevertheless, contemporary research suggests that dispensing advice within psychotherapy can be beneficial, contingent on factors such as cultural and social context, as well as the characteristics of both the client and therapist (Duan et al., 2018). On the authority of Tameem ibn Aus ad-Daree, the Prophet (ﷺ) said, "'The *deen* (religion) is *naseehah* (advice, sincerity).' We said, 'To whom?' He (ﷺ) said, 'To Allāh, His Book, His Messenger, and to the

leaders of the Muslims and their common folk'"
(Muslim (a)).

Al-Ghazālī identified certain characteristics that
should be present in such a person, emphasising
the importance of

- "Uprightness in character
- Companionship to foster a collaborative rather
  than hierarchical relationship
- Scholarship with a strong foundational understanding of the intricate process of facilitating
  change" (Al-Ghazālī, 2014, p. 257).

Al-Ghazālī further explains that the practitioner
may sometimes help individuals identify psychological or behavioural tendencies of which they were
previously unaware or prescribe exercises to promote personal insight (Al-Ghazālī, 2014). Rassool
(2023) proposed that "In order to produce the
highest quality Islāmic psychotherapists and counsellors, it is important to have a synthesis of faith
(*iman*), knowledge (*ilm*), good character (*akhlaq*),
and the qualities of the 'master' therapist" (p. 97).

In contrast to certain contemporary psychological
models that primarily concentrate on cognitive
aspects, the emphasis of the Islāmic psychotherapist
and mental healthcare practitioner is centred around
the spiritual heart (*qalb*) of individuals. Therefore,
the practitioner's role and interaction with the
client revolves around recognising the condition of
the heart, as it serves as a site where both the client
and the therapist can exhibit signs of well-being or
dysfunction (Kershavazi et al., 2020). Apart from

possessing these qualities, it is crucial for practitioners to construct an effective case formulation that reflects an understanding of the Islāmic ontology of human nature. This includes identifying and addressing any deficiencies in the client's psyche in order to establish appropriate treatment goals. Furthermore, therapists should have knowledge of the behavioural literature on the psychology of spirituality. This familiarity enables them to be well-versed in spiritually oriented interventions that can impact psychological well-being (Vieten et al., 2013).

An essential aspect of the practitioner's role is assisting the client in gaining self-awareness and reflecting this insight as a clear mirror. In order to provide an accurate reflection for the client, the practitioner must also purify and refine the mirror of their own heart. It is important for the therapist to genuinely care for the well-being of the client and strive to facilitate treatment that is in their best interests. While the practitioner is skilled in guiding individuals through the process of self-discovery, establishing a strong therapeutic rapport is another crucial element of effective clinical practice (Leach, 2005). The Prophet Muhammad (ﷺ) stated: Whoever relieves a Muslim of a burden from the burdens of the world, Allāh will relieve him of a burden from the burdens on the Day of Judgment. And whoever helps ease a difficulty in this world, Allāh will grant him ease from a difficulty in the world and in the Hereafter and whoever conceals (the faults of) a Muslim, Allāh will cover (his faults) in the world and the Hereafter. And Allāh is engaged in helping the worshipper as long as the worshipper is engaged in helping his brother" (Tirmidhi (a)).

Additionally, it is crucial for the practitioner to adopt a flexible approach in treating their clients. This involves recognising that there may be alternative explanations for the nature of the problem and being open to incorporating Islāmic-based healing practices. Frank and Frank (1991) suggest that all major healing approaches, including psychotherapy, share common characteristics, such as establishing an emotionally invested relationship between the client and practitioner, describing the client's symptoms, and agreeing upon a healing process that is determined and accepted by both parties. Therefore, it is essential for the practitioner to view themselves as an instrument of Allāh's destiny (*qadr*) for the individual seeking help and to be grateful for the role they have been given (Kershavazi et al., 2020).

The practitioner should embody kindness and compassion, taking into account the needs and emotions of those under their care, recognising that it is a gift and trust *(amanah)* bestowed upon them by God. This quality was exemplified by the Prophet Muhammad (ﷺ), as mentioned in the Qur'ān:

فَبِمَا رَحْمَةٍ مِّنَ ٱللَّهِ لِنتَ لَهُمْ ۖ وَلَوْ كُنتَ فَظًّا غَلِيظَ ٱلْقَلْبِ لَٱنفَضُّواْ مِنْ حَوْلِكَ ۖ فَٱعْفُ عَنْهُمْ وَٱسْتَغْفِرْ لَهُمْ وَشَاوِرْهُمْ فِى ٱلْأَمْرِ

- *So, by mercy from God, [O Muhammad], you were lenient with them. And if you had been rude [in speech] and harsh in heart, they would have disbanded from about you. So, pardon them and ask forgiveness for them and consult them in the matter. And when you have decided, then rely upon God. Indeed, God loves those who rely [upon Him].* (Al -Imran 3:159, interpretation of the meaning)

Challenges and recommendations

Seeking treatment for physical or mental ailments is not seen as conflicting with seeking assistance from Alláh (Rassool, 2019). However, due to beliefs in *jinn* possession, witchcraft, and the evil eye, many Muslims do not seek help from psychological or psychiatric services. Moreover, there is hesitancy and caution among Muslims when it comes to seeking support from mental health professionals. This reluctance is attributed to a lack of under-standing of Islām and concerns that the treatment methods may not align with their religious beliefs (Rassool, 2019). In addition, many individuals who seek spiritual treatment initially engage in methods or approaches that do not align with Islāmic princi-ples and later discover therapies and treatments that are grounded in and endorsed by the Islāmic tradi-tion such as *adkhaar* (remembrances), *ruqyah-ash-Shar'iah*, and *tibb-an-nabawi*. The significance of integrating spirituality into the healing process has thus become evident. Muslim practitioners ought to ponder about questions such as how would the Prophet (ﷺ) have advised in such situations? How can we incorporate a spiritual dimension while addressing the necessary psychological aspects?

The recognition of the importance of the spiritual self, particularly the soul, becomes indisputable. This highlights the necessity of incorporating "spiritual treatment modalities" as an integral part of a comprehensive therapeutic plan within the broader Muslim community's therapeutic framework.

Although challenging, it is important to address these areas of concern. Muslim practitioners will need to assess the client's cultural identity, worldview, and religious spirituality. This will ensure that interventions are culturally and religiously sensitive and considerate of the individual's beliefs and values (Rassool & Sange, 2014). According to Koenig et al. (1996), some Muslim clients may present with mental health issues that have a psycho-spiritual element, requiring a comprehensive and holistic spiritual assessment. This assessment serves to acknowledge the significance of religion in the client's life and identify potential coping resources. Rassool (2019) emphasises the importance of including this assessment by considering factors such as understanding the client's worldview and their beliefs regarding the causes of health and illness, establishing the connection between the presenting problem and the spiritual realm, and enabling informed decision-making regarding religious and spiritual interventions.

It is well accepted in the Islāmic tradition that detachment from Allāh or a lack of remembrance and awareness of Allāh often underlie discontent, despair, and psychological struggles, increasing and amplifying over time. While the prevalence and severity of clinical conditions, manifestations, and pathologies remain a crucial concern, disconnection from Allāh and different types of afflictions significantly exacerbates these issues and, in many instances, may play a fundamental role in spiritual ailments. Allah says:

وَمَنْ أَعْرَضَ عَن ذِكْرِى فَإِنَّ لَهُ مَعِيشَةً ضَنكًا وَنَحْشُرُهُ يَوْمَ ٱلْقِيَـٰمَةِ أَعْمَىٰ

- *And whoever turns away from My remembrance – indeed, he will have a depressed [i.e., difficult] life, and We will gather [i.e., raise] him on the Day of Resurrection blind.* (Taha 20:124, interpretation of the meaning)

Conclusion

The Islāmic tradition has always aimed at incorporating the body, mind, and soul. In Islām, the family or social system is given much importance (Rassool & Sange, 2014).The rise of modern psychology in the West differs from this perspective and often disregards the notion of religious values and community support. This has led to a reactive approach towards mental health issues, with many individuals becoming dependent on psychologists, counsellors, and medication due to diminished social supportive systems. Modern psychology's narrow focus on the individual without considering their family or community and spiritual belief systems causes limitations to the therapeutic process (Rassool & Sange, 2014).

According to Rassool and Sange (2014), Islām does not distinguish between psychological and spiritual well-being, as both are interconnected. The way health and illness are explained is influenced by an individual's broader belief system and values. This understanding significantly shapes the approach to interventions. It is essential for Muslim practitioners to provide personalised treatment plans for their clients, avoiding a one-size-fits-all approach, as each client has unique circumstances. It is also necessary for the practitioner to be aware of the stigmas and reservations with regards to mainstream psychology and Muslim clients. The more resources, knowledge, and tools Muslim practitioners have at their disposal, particularly from an Islāmic-based approach, the better equipped they will be to respond to their clients' individual needs and concerns. This will enable them to genuinely assist their clients in achieving transformation and healing at a deep and meaningful level (Hecker & Kottler, 2002b). We as Islāmic psychotherapists and mental health practitioners bear the responsibility for both identifying and addressing challenges, as well as finding solutions for them.

References

Abdussalam Bali, W. (2015). *The cutting edge: How to face evil sorcerers* (H. Kreidly, Trans.). UK: Dar Al Kotob Al-Ilmiyah.

Abu Dāwūd. *Sunan Abu Dawud.* 3874. In-book reference: Book 29, Hadīth 20. English translation: Book 28, Hadīth 3865.

Abū Dāwūd, S. (2009). *Sunan Abū Dāwūd.* Beirut: Dār al-Rasā'il al-'Ā lamiyyah.

Al-Ghazālī. (2014). *Al-Ghazālī on the treatment of the heart: The spiritual teachings of Abu Hamid Al-Ghazālī* (W. J. Winter, Trans.). UK: Kube Publishing.

Al Jeraisy, K. (n.d.). *Self ruqya treatment: Do it yourself, treat your family.* (M. A. M. Mohamed, Trans.). Saudi Arabia: The Believers Provision Series Book 5.

Duan, Y., Lu, L., Chen, J., Wu, C., Liang, J., Zheng, Y., Wu, J., Rong, P., & Tang, C. (2018). *Psychosocial interventions for Alzheimers disease cognitive symptoms: A Bayesian network meta-analysis. 18*(1), 175.

Frank, J. D., & Frank, J. B. (1991). *Persuasion and healing: A comparative study of psychotherapy.* Baltimore, Maryland, US: JHU Press.

Hecker, L. L., & Kottler, J. A. (2002a). Growing creative therapists. Introduction to a special issue. *Journal of Clinical Activities, Assignments & Handouts in Psychotherapy* (2), 1–3.

Hecker, L. L., & Kottler, J. A. (2002b). Islām and clinical practice: Guidelines for psychotherapists and counselors. In A. E. Kazdin (Ed.), *Handbook of clinical psychology: Theory, research, and practice* (pp. 791–806). New Jersey: John Wiley & Sons.

Ibn Hibban. (1993). *Sahih Ibn Hibban bi-Tartib Ibn Bilban.* (S. al-Arna'ut, Ed. 2). Beirut: Mu'assassat al-Risalah.

Al-Jawziyyah, I.A.Q (n.d.). *Spiritual disease and its cure: An adequate reply to whomsoever asks for curative medicines for sins* (Z. Amiraat, Ed.). London: Al Firdous LTD.

Joshanloo, M. (2013). A comparison of Western and Islāmic conceptions of happiness. *Journal of Happiness Studies*, 14(6), 1857–1874.

Kershavazi, H., Khan, F., Ali, B., & Awaad, R. (2020). *Applying Islāmic principles to clinical mental health care. Introducing traditional Islāmic integrated psychotherapy.* New York: Routledge.

Kershavazi, N., Deuraseh, N., & Moshtagh, S. (2020). *Islāmic psychology and mental health: An emerging field. In Islāmic psychotherapy: Theory and practice.* 33–52. New York: Routledge.

Koenig, H. G., Larson, D. B., & Matthews, D. A. (1996). Religion and psychotherapy with older adults. *Journal of Geriatric Psychiatry*, 29, 2, 155–174.

Leach, M. J. (2005). *Rapport: A key to treatment success* (4), 262–265.

Leach, M. M. (2005). Building rapport with clients: A practical guide to gaining therapeutic presence. *Journal of Clinical Psychology*, 61(4), 511–524.

Rahman, F. (1987). *Health and medicine in the Islāmic tradition*. New York: The Crossroad Publishing Company.

Rassool, G. Hussein, & Sange, C. (2014). *Chapter 6: Islāmic belief affecting healthcare*, In G. Hussein Rassool (Ed.), *Cultural competence in caring for Muslim clients*. Basingstoke, Hampshire: Palgrave Macmillan.

Rassool, G. Hussein. (2016). *Islāmic counselling: An introduction to theory and practice*. Hove, East Sussex: Routledge.

Rassool, G. Hussein. (2019). *Evil eye, jinn possession, and mental health issues: An Islāmic perspective*. (1st ed.). Oxford: Routledge.

Rassool, G. Hussein. (2023). *Islāmic psychology. The basics*. Oxford: Routledge.

Tirmidhi, *Jami at Tirmidhi.*1930. In-book reference: Book 27, Hadīth 36. English translation: Vol. 4, Book 1, Hadīth 1930.

Vieten, C., Scammel, S., Pilato, R., Ammondson, I., Pargament, K. I., & Lukoff, D. (2013). *Spiritual and religious competencies for psychologists*, 1–16.

Index

For Product Safety Concerns and Information please contact our EU
representative GPSR@taylorandfrancis.com
Taylor & Francis Verlag GmbH, Kaufingerstraße 24, 80331 München, Germany